Angel Classics

Horace

PIERRE CORNEILLE (1606-84) was a lawyer who served for some twenty years in Normandy's courts in Rouen. In the 1630s he enjoyed the patronage of Richelieu as a dramatist, his reputation being built at first on comedies. His tragicomedy *Le Cid* (1637), an extraordinary success with the public, aroused intense controversy in literary circles. He went on to write *Horace* (1640), *Cinna* (1641) and *Polyeucte* (1643), works of major importance in the formation of French classical tragedy.

A prolific playwright, Corneille continued to write serious plays, but after the civil war during Louis XIV's minority known as the Fronde, public taste for heroic tragedy waned. Corneille ceased to write for the stage for seven years, and when he next did, he was largely eclipsed by a younger generation of dramatists, among them Racine.

Corneille created a new type of historical drama in France, of great psychological depth, structured round conflicts between private and public morality. His eloquent and memorable rhetoric works powerfully with brilliant dramaturgical skills.

ALAN BROWNJOHN is the author of nine books of poems and two novels. With his wife Sandy Brownjohn he has translated Goethe's *Torquato Tasso* (broadcast on BBC Radio 3, performed at the National Theatre, and published by Angel Books in 1985) and edited three secondary school teaching anthologies. He was Chairman of the Poetry Society from 1982 to 1988. He has written and reviewed regularly for the *Times Literary Supplement*, the *New Statesman* and the *Sunday Times*, and has been a frequent contributor to BBC radio poetry programmes.

DAVID R. CLARKE, MA, PHD, is a Senior Lecturer in French at King's College London. He is the author of *Pierre Corneille: Poetics and Political Drama under Louis XIII* (Cambridge University Press, 1992).

PIERRE CORNEILLE

Horace

Translated by ALAN BROWNJOHN

Introduction and notes by David Clarke

ANGEL BOOKS
London

First published in 1996 by
Angel Books, 3 Kelross Road, London N5 2QS
1 3 5 7 9 10 8 6 4 2

British Library Cataloguing in Publication data:
A catalogue record for this book is available from the British Library
ISBN 0 946162 57 3 pbk

This book is printed on Permanent Paper conforming to the British Library
recommendations and to the full American standard

∞

Funded by
THE
ARTS
COUNCIL
OF ENGLAND

This book is also supported by the French Ministry for Foreign Affairs, as
part of the Burgess Programme headed for the French Embassy in London
by the Institut Français du Royaume-Uni

institut français

Typeset in Great Britain by
Metropress (Type) Ltd, Wellingborough, Northants
Printed and bound by
Woolnough Bookbinding Ltd, Irthlingborough, Northants

Contents

Translator's Preface

The alexandrine couplets in French classical tragedy are virtually impossible to copy in English, certainly not in a way that makes them convincing for stage use. I have rendered Corneille's verse not with his own six stresses and twelve syllables, but in a five-stress English blank verse line mostly containing rather more syllables than an iambic pentameter, so the individual feet often become something other than strict iambs. The aim has been to allow this flexible line to accommodate all of the meaning contained in the hexameter of the original; to make it speakable for actors; and to preserve as far as possible the frequently significant order of the words in Corneille's line, balance and antithesis being important elements in his rhyming couplets.

Another purpose throughout this translation has been to deliver accurately as much as is practical of the rhetorical power of the original, in modern English which has a degree of formality and dignity appropriate to Corneille's tragedy. In places liberties have been taken to bring the utterances of certain characters closer to modern rhetorical usage. But this is not a colloquial updating of the play or its ideas. It needs no alteration or modernisation. Much in the theme, action and rhetoric of *Horace* will be only too terrifyingly and poignantly familiar from recent experience.

A. B.

Introduction

by David Clarke

Pierre Corneille (1606-84) was a lawyer who served from 1628 to 1650 in Normandy's courts of law in Rouen. By March 1640, when *Horace* was first performed in Paris, he also had a considerable reputation as a dramatist. The successful author of six comedies, one tragedy and two tragicomedies, he had enjoyed five years of patronage and financial support from Cardinal Richelieu, Louis XIII's first minister and effective ruler of France. However, the extraordinary success of *Le Cid* in early 1637 had provoked a bruising literary squabble with rival dramatists such as Scudéry and Mairet. This developed into a broader and acrimonious debate over the poetic and political proprieties to be observed in the writing of serious drama. In January 1639 Chapelain, Secretary of the Académie Française[1] and the expert who had sought to end the controversy by publishing the Académie's verdict on the play, reported that Corneille seemed quite discouraged from writing again for the stage.

Corneille was undoubtedly upset by the ways in which Aristotle's *Poetics* had been used to criticise his play. This text had been rediscovered over a century earlier and had been much commented on, principally by Italian theorists. Interest in poetics had vigorously revived in France during the 1630s and, whatever the differences over Aristotle, everyone including Corneille was agreed that to create a successful imitation of life the poet should model his practice on that of Classical Antiquity. Aristotle's *Poetics*, in discussing the epic and tragedy, observes that all poetry deals in truths 'more philosophical than those of history' and goes on to discuss how that higher significance derives from the tragic poet's skilful observation of certain formal constraints as he selected and 'properly' ordered the source material he imitated. So too the Classical French dramatist's primary concern was to shape particular historical events so that their stage representation offered the audience a coherent and moving spectacle capable of universal moral application.

The debate over the rights and wrongs of *Le Cid* was a watershed in this literary debate over 'proper' poetic imitation, and Corneille's response to it in writing *Horace* helped to establish the value and effectiveness of Classical 'regularity'. The play offers a good early example of the intellectual focus and emotional force that seventeenth-century French dramatists achieved by observing the Classical 'rules' and conventions. Of these the most celebrated were the three unities: of action (that there be but a single and complete action to which everything in the play contributes), of time (that the dramatic action cover a period of no more than twenty-four hours), and of place (that the dramatic action occur in a single location). These unities, together with the twin organising principles of balance and contrast, work to formidable effect in *Horace*, as Corneille selects and orders his historical material, occasionally even altering events the better to serve a dramatic argument that sets public glory and political ambition tragically at odds with the private world of personal ties and individual hopes of happiness.

More contentious than the argument over formal regularity was the debate over the 'morality' of tragedy and whether the seventeenth-century dramatist should do more than simply entertain. Should he, for instance, make his own contribution to public order by censoring his historical material and presenting only an exemplary image of human behaviour? Here Corneille was at odds with the semi-official view that the poet, in the interests of social order and public education, should at least edit the truth or, better, entirely avoid any subject at variance with conventional morality. He had already been censured on this issue, since, according to the Académie's verdict, the heroine of *Le Cid* set 'a very bad example' by still loving the man who had killed her father and even agreeing to marry him in the final scene of the play. In turning for his new play to pre-Republican Roman history, Corneille had chosen no less contentious material. The legend concerned events during the reign of Tullus Hostilius: two sets of brothers, the three Horatii and the three Curiatii, ignored the closest ties of kinship in fighting a triple combat to decide a war between Rome and Alba; the Horatius who was the single survivor of that combat then killed his sister Camilla for mourning the Curiatius to whom she was betrothed (Livy, *History of Rome*, Book I, 23-6). Small wonder then that, when in February 1640 he gave a private reading of *Horace* before an expert assembly, serious criticisms were expressed and some critics even seemed prepared to reopen hostilities. With characteristic independence of mind, Corneille presented *Horace* unchanged to the Paris theatre-goers and its success silenced his critics. As one wit put it in a parody of Livy, 'The Duumvirs condemned *Horace* but the people acquitted him.' Yet greater success followed with two more 'Roman' tragedies, *Cinna* (1641) and *Polyeucte* (1643), and over the next thirty years Corneille went on to write fifteen more historical tragedies, gaining a reputation as a master-dramatist whom his contemporaries ranked with the greatest tragedians of Antiquity.

Fully to understand the immediate reasons for the success of *Horace* in 1640 we need to look to the contemporary political context. Corneille's choice of a Roman historical subject fully conformed with his powerful patron's encouragement of serious drama based on Roman history, the better to illuminate the moral and political significance of France's direct involvement since 1635 in the Thirty Years War. Sabina's anachronistic reference to Gibraltar and the Rhine (I.1.47-51) makes it clear that this play about Rome's first step on the road to dominion of the world invites flattering parallels between the military achievements of ancient Rome and contemporary French ambitions in Europe in opposition to Habsburg Spain and Austria. Since Corneille dedicated *Horace* to Richelieu with fulsome expressions of indebtedness to his patron's 'great ideas', and since Julia, Horatius and Old Horatius all insist so resoundingly on the need for total devotion to the national interest, it is often argued that the play supports the Cardinal's belligerent 'policy of glory'. Certainly its repeated allusions to Rome's glorious future seem confidently to anticipate French success in the current rivalry for European dominance, and the Cardinal's political realism is reflected in Tullus's verdict in Act V, which holds that broader interests of state justify some relaxation of the law. Above all, Richelieu might well have appreciated the assertion that, in recognition of that national interest, great servants of the state – like the Cardinal himself – are not to be judged, much less condemned, according to the laws that govern common men.

Such connections may be made, but the reality of 1640 was that Richelieu's policy of war was far from popular. French military engagements had been conducted with more fanfares than success, and the Cardinal would have to wait until a few months before his death in late 1642 to hear of victories that justified a costly war. In the meantime his official apologists urged unquestioning acceptance of repressive policies and ever-increasing taxation at home. Not all were persuaded, however, either in Paris or in the provinces. In July 1639 the peasantry of Corneille's own Normandy marched on Rouen to protest against increased taxation. The very existence of government-led attempts to use the public stage to educate the public in favourite political 'truths' also reminds us that *Horace* was probably applauded by a fair proportion of spectators who were unpleasantly aware of the cost of military ambition, whether they were aristocrats who disliked the repressiveness of the present government or humbler folk increasingly pressed by the rising burden of taxation. The war was also unpopular for more principled reasons as far as 'good Catholic' Frenchmen were concerned. French foreign policy prior to Richelieu's control of the King's Council had favoured a 'Catholic' alliance with Spain. Thus Louis XIII's queen was Anne of Austria, Habsburg daughter of Philip III of Spain and Margaret of Austria, herself sister to the Habsburg Holy Roman Emperor Ferdinand II. So too Anne's brother, Philip IV of Spain, was married to Elizabeth of Bourbon, sister of her husband Louis XIII. Richelieu's foreign policy, however, being intended to destroy what risked becoming a Habsburg hegemony in Europe, scandalously set good Catholics at each other's throats and divided even the King's own family. Anne's position at the French court was certainly a very difficult one, and some even suggested – quite without foundation – that she had betrayed state secrets to her husband's Habsburg enemies.

Personal patronage in the reign of Louis XIII did not necessarily entail propagandist subservience, and Corneille's dedication of

Horace manages to combine flattery with an independence of mind reflected in a play which never unconditionally celebrates military glory. Indeed, the major disadvantage of too simplifying a triumphalist and 'patriotic' reading of *Horace* is not only that it is selective in its appeal to contemporary realities but that it ignores the personal tragedy of Horatius himself. It forgets that, at any performance of *Horace*, it is quite impossible to listen only to those Roman voices who confidently predict future glory and remain indifferent to the suffering of others who wait upon events over which they have no control. If, on the other hand, we pay due attention to those less belligerent voices – and at a performance of the play it is impossible not to do so – we shall begin to understand the success of Corneille's tragedy in 1640 and why it still has the power to challenge and disturb modern audiences with its exploration of the problematic relationship between violence and valour and of the cost of national glory. And here it is notable how effectively the Classical conventions of 'regularity' work to establish a moral breadth and tragic focus which a one-sided interpretation of the play fails to recognise. From the start the unity of place establishes a polarity between private and public experience. By setting the entire action in the house of the Horatii, Corneille focuses our attention on the way major political decisions and military events offstage affect the closer bonds of a single extended family. The dominant perspective, then, is that of a family embattled within a city which itself is at war with another city. Only in the last act does that outside political world physically enter the private domestic context when King Tullus, supreme representative of the collective interest, passes judgement on a husband and brother who has killed his own kith and kin in unswerving dedication to the future glory of Rome.

Discreet alterations to historical fact also humanise and sharpen the impact of the drama. Corneille reduces the number of brothers on each side to a single representative, but adds two more female roles to create three admirably contrasted parts, all expressing very different assessments of Rome's ambitions. The invented minor role of Julia uncompromisingly urges sacrifice of all personal feelings to the warlike pursuit of imperial glory (I.1.20-2), thus announcing Horatius's and Old Horatius's characteristically Roman dedication to the City and its glorious destiny. No less single-mindedly Camilla sets out the claims of individual happiness, giving absolute priority to her love for Curiatius. Finally, the invented role of Sabina, wife to Horatius and sister of Curiatius, tightens yet further the bonds that link the two families, and this in turn heightens the atrocity of the demands that will later be made on the younger men in the name of love of country. This part has been criticised as both ineffectual and wordy, perhaps justifiably so in the case of Sabina's request to die in place of her husband in V.3. But we should not forget that Sabina's dual identity as Alban daughter and Roman wife makes it impossible for her to take sides and so find a way into the action. Indeed, it is precisely this combination of impotence with eloquence that makes the role so illuminating. Impossibly torn in her loyalties, she can only speak for the sufferings of a common humanity overtaken by the enormity of war. This she does with an eloquence which gives her almost a choral function in the play as she clarifies our understanding of the action, situating present events within the broader perspectives of Rome's imperial destiny, ironising bitterly about Rome's brutal demands on her citizens, or protesting against the cruel incomprehensibility of gods who permit a conflict which contravenes their own laws. Even as she opens the play by acknowledging that the gods have ordained that Rome will rule the world (I.39-44), she confronts us with a reminder that this glorious destiny will only be achieved within a peculiarly Roman tradition of sacrificial violence. In a fine illustration of how effectively the twenty-four hour convention can compress the action and yet accommodate the widest temporal perspectives, she measures the significance of what is to come by recalling the 'original sin' of Rome's foundation. Romulus, the Alban prince who founded Rome, murdered his brother Remus and raised its walls over his brother's body. Once again the sinister tradition will recur in a matricidal victory of Rome over her mother city Alba (I.1.53-6). And with that observation Sabina prepares us for a tragic day of triumph and disaster during which the same crime will be repeated six more times.[2] This enormity lays bare the central paradox of Corneille's tragedy as Sabina tries in vain to comprehend how gods who are the final guarantors of justice can give their blessing to this Roman tradition of unnatural crime (I.1.41-4). In that mystery lies the source of Horatius's future tragedy, and Tullus will remind us of that in the last moments of the play (V.3.1755-8), as Rome marches on towards a glorious empire won by force of arms. In similar manner Camilla's prophetic curse directs our attention even beyond that apogee of Imperial Roman power with the reminder that even Rome will fall victim to civil war and be sacked by barbarian invaders (IV.5.1305-12).

These repeated references to the epic story of Rome's rise and fall enlarge the significance of the action and make of Horatius's triumph and disgrace an exemplary illustration of the splendours and miseries of all human endeavour. Destiny, the active manifestation of the inscrutable purposes of the gods, has prepared a test of courage for Horatius and Curiatius, as they agree when confronted with the news that they have been chosen to fight (II.3.431-4). In assuming the heroic responsibility of furthering that mysterious providential purpose they must embrace present necessity and seize the chance of earning universal admiration by displaying in action the qualities they know themselves to possess. If the demands made on them seem exceptionally harsh then so much the better, for only by overcoming exceptional difficulties can they show exceptional valour and claim their place within the march of history (II.3.437-52). Here once again Corneille tidies up his historical sources to ensure a consistent and striking contrast between Roman and Alban values. In Livy and Dionysius the Albans are the first to sever all personal links with their friends and adversaries; the Romans follow suit. Corneille reverses this priority in the exchanges between Horatius and Curiatius and thereby creates a formidable dramatic contrast of values. In response to Curiatius's distaste for the ruthless civism of Rome, Horatius parades a 'Roman' disregard for all ties of natural affection, reducing his friend to no more than his Alban opponent. For all that Curiatius will ultimately only be able to fight Horatius in just such a perspective, his anguished reply has provoked spontaneous applause ever since the play's first performance, so effectively does its humanity voice a characteristically Alban respect for the natural ties of affection and reverence for Natural Law:

> HORATIUS: *You are Alba's choice, and I no longer know you.*
> CURIATIUS: *I still know you, which is why my heart is breaking.*
> (II.3.502-3)

Given such clear-cut differences in the moral values specific to their respective origins, the prospect of fratricidal combat is received very differently by the two men. Horatius has no qualms about a confrontation the conditions of which, in calling on him to set aside the bonds of kinship, perfectly accord with 'Roman' values. For him the triple combat offers an unequalled opportunity to show his Roman *vertu* (manly courage) in unflinching devotion to the City's pursuit of military glory (II.3.489-94). For Curiatius, that fratricidal fight to the death for supremacy offends all Alban values since it involves a deliberate rejection of the sacred bonds of kinship. If he expresses regret in accepting the necessity to fight this is because, although he too shares in a heroic ambition to distinguish himself, he cannot reconcile that ambition with the morality of the combat which the gods have thrust upon him. Thus, in a typically Cornelian illustration of the tragic paradoxes of heroic freedom and political constraint, both young men freely choose to fight but are forced to choose since, whether they call it the gods or their political circumstances, a tragic destiny forces that choice upon them. The following scenes make this painfully clear, as Camilla's hope that Curiatius will refuse to fight is quickly disappointed, and Sabina's scathing attacks on such heroic dedication to country make the young men waver for only a moment before Old Horatius stiffens their resolve and, once again, reduces the women to despair.

Corneille's brilliant use of suspense was later to become his trademark as a dramatist, and the highly dramatic series of shocks and reversals that he contrives in Acts III and IV serves once again to illustrate the impenetrability of gods who, to the uncomprehending despair of the women, constantly intervene in the action. Just as the oracle's promise of peace and happiness in Act I (I.2.195-8) now seems a cruel mockery (III.1.760-2), so Corneille's invention of a truce and consultation of the gods through augury raises hopes (III.2.828-30) only to dash them again when the gods permit a fratricidal combat the prospect of which horrifies even hardened soldiers (III.2.785-92). Sabina and Camilla abandon all hope (III.5.932-4) only to hope again when Julia's false report of Horatius's flight reduces Old Horatius to despair but permits the mistaken belief that at least their men are safe. Yet again, however, events offstage confound the women, as Valerius opens Act IV with a true account of the combat. Here, and in careful coherence with his play's depiction of Roman values, Corneille's narrative is even more shocking than Livy's. As a culminating act of patriotic devotion cheered to the heavens by the Romans, Corneille's Horatius makes a human sacrifice, triumphantly dedicating the last of his opponents to the future success of Rome (IV.2.1131-3). Old Horatius's delight at this victory, which bereaves the helpless women of brothers and lover, leads remorselessly to the well-meaning insensitivity of his and Horatius's 'Roman' advice that they abandon private grief for public rejoicing. This in turn drives Camilla to revolt against a city that has so brutally set the pursuit of power and glory over her claims to individual happiness (IV.5.1298-1318).

Here too, dramatic intensity is served by the way in which the unity of place requires that Horatius return from the battlefield to meet his sister in the heart of his family. In place of a chance meeting at the gates of Rome, Corneille devises a confrontation between Horatius and Camilla who is bent on a deliberately suicidal revolt against the mother city. In yet another crucial modification of the record, Horatius does not kill her in anger. Instead he kills her in a principled 'act of justice' (IV.6.1323) inspired by a Roman 'reason' which must take precedence over a brother's patience for his tearful sister (IV.5.1319). This fundamentally important change underlines yet again the ideological consistency of Corneille's Horatius as he moves from public to private violence. Furthermore, Corneille's determination to show this killing almost on stage – a scandal prohibited by the stage conventions of the time – indicates how important it was that his audience be spared nothing of the inhumanity enshrined in the Roman concept of *virtus* (French *vertu*, in Corneille's usage, often has the sense of vigour in pursuit of chosen ends). Unhappily, some twenty years later, Corneille wrote an *Examen* of *Horace* in which he seems to have lost sight of the challenging political argument of his own play.[3] Part of this short critique reflects theoretical debates peculiar to the 1660s, and Corneille seems over-fastidious in his regrets at having submitted Horatius to a double peril, since he moves from one danger (the combat) to a second (the risk of being punished by death for killing Camilla). This concern for a technical flaw entirely ignores the natural impetus of the play in performance, for Horatius's second violent suppression of an enemy of Rome inevitably prompts our curiosity about the consequences of such a deed. And in effect, when Horatius faces the shocked reactions of his family and responds to Sabina's disgust by a restatement of Roman principles she cannot and will not embrace, the play reaches a moment of tension which can be resolved only in a concluding exploration of the significance of all that has gone before.

The last act opens with another sobering insight into the severity of Roman patriotism, even within the household. Old Horatius privately admits to his son that Camilla deserved to die for her sacrilege in cursing Rome but indicates that he, as head of the family, should have been the one to punish her. On Tullus's entry this question of authority is given political development by Valerius, who accuses Horatius of usurping Tullus's powers and acting with a ruthlessness incompatible with the survival of Rome itself. Once called to defend himself, Horatius refuses to do so since, by his Roman lights, he has committed no offence. He simply asks that he may take his life to avoid further humiliation as he measures the extent of his fall from general acclaim into present ignominy and incomprehension. He has lost everything but the inner certainty of his personal integrity in his bitter meditation on how time and circumstance have worked to destroy his earlier hopes. But his tragedy is still not complete, for the rift widens yet further between himself and those he served so selflessly when his wife and his father try to deny him the death he seeks, the first by offering her life in expiation of a crime he does not acknowledge, the second by asserting, against his private belief, that Horatius is innocent because he killed Camilla on impulse. Finally Tullus, in whose wisdom and understanding Horatius alone trusts, completes the hero's misfortune. Speaking for the city to whose interests Horatius has sacrificed everything, he disregards Horatius's request to die and disowns a sacrificial devotion which Rome had earlier applauded in the triple combat and which remains the essential condition of its future triumphs. Recoiling from the stark consequences of Horatius's Roman *virtus*, which so brutally sacrifices the individual to interest of state, Tullus prefers the convenient fiction offered by Old Horatius and unhesitatingly judges Camilla's death an impulsive crime so unnatural as to shock even the gods. But even as he condemns Horatius, Tullus recalls for the last time that those same gods sanctioned fratricidal violence in Rome's blood beginnings.

Calling on Rome to avert its eyes once more from that equivocal violence which stands behind the City's ascent to power, he sets Rome's saviour above the laws that govern lesser mortals and enlists him once more in the service of the City. With that unwanted pardon the new King of Rome and Alba abjures and recuperates the sacrificial devotion which won him two crowns, and with formidable political realism condemns Horatius to live for Rome once more.

Even nineteenth-century Frenchmen found Horatius an uncomfortably ruthless hero. Rather than modify his reading of the play as a celebration of public conscience over private feeling, the theatre critic Sarcey promoted Old Horatius to principal 'patriotic' hero. Matters had not changed much by the 1930s, when a distinguished author and critic – later shot for collaboration – seemed to see in Horatius a prefiguration of National Socialist devotion to the Fatherland.[4] Indeed, a one-sided 'duty over love' reading still continues in many French school-classes. The result is that generations of schoolchildren, after indoctrination and unhappy exposure to improving matinées of Cornelian tragedy, grow up unshakably convinced that *Horace* advocates a chillingly superhuman victory of duty over passion in unswerving service of country. More thoughtfully, a Danish observer of political events in the years leading up to the Second World War held that *Horace* offered a judgement on patriotism once it degenerated into chauvinism.[5] But only after the Nazi occupation of France and in the aftermath of the Second World War did discussion of Corneille really come to life. One French scholar wrote eloquently about it as a tragic illustration of idealism betrayed.[6] Others looked variously to late feudal values,[7] to Nietzsche,[8] to seventeenth-century Neo-Stoicism and Jesuit moral theology,[9] or to the Hegelian master-slave dialectic,[10] all as keys to an understanding of Corneille's tragic heroes. More recently still, young Americans, due to be drafted to Vietnam and acutely aware of the problematic morality of such neo-colonial conflict, discovered in *Horace* a tragic demystification of the patriotic call to arms and honourable violence in circumstances which dishonoured the very values they were held to be defending. As one critic memorably wrote: '*Horace* turns to the extreme case in order to define the limits and essence of patriotism . . . To understand patriotism we must strip away its blandly pious garb of everyday: we must lay bare the terrible paradox, the impious piety hidden in its heart.'[11]

Some element of truth exists in all these readings, for there never was a dramatist more even-handed in the eloquence and force he gave to his various characters as they speak for the values by which they live and die. For all that Corneille expressed some misgivings in his *Examen* of 1660 about the debates that make up the final act of *Horace*, that act provides a fitting conclusion to a play that admirably illustrates the importance of the word in French Classical tragedy. D'Aubignac, a contemporary theoretician, famously observed that, on the stage, 'speech is action', and indeed this holds true of *Horace*, not only of Valerius's vivid narration of the combat (IV.2). Words, like actions, cannot be withdrawn (the confrontation between Horatius and Curiatius in II.3); like actions they provoke to action (Camilla's curse in IV.5), and even more effectively than actions they betray our hopes and destroy cherished ideals (Tullus's final judgement in V.3). Forensic and rhetorical, Corneille's poetry is the poetry of debate, of sharp and impassioned argument the expression of which is admirably adjusted to the enactment of seemingly insoluble conflicts of characters passionately committed to their chosen values. In this sense the carefully orchestrated tirades and verbal passages of arms that structure Corneille's tragedy work less to force our judgement than to prompt us into anxious reflection. The poetic communication of feeling in Racine's tragedies of passion is undoubtedly more immediately moving in so far as it makes a direct appeal to our emotions. In contrast Corneille, as Sartre observed,[12] is less interested in character than in myth, and the sober clarity and strength of his poetry perfectly serves a tragedy which, in addressing itself first to our understanding, leads us through awed comprehension of our political condition towards a final and piercing experience of the pity of things.

At the public level *Horace* even-handedly reflects all the exhilarations and glory of military ambition and forcefully demonstrates the tainted character of any political order that sacrifices its own humanity to the pursuit of power. At the level of private experience the play's disturbing exploration of greatness misdirected marks out the heights and limits of individual heroic self-fulfilment. But in the fullness with which it expresses all sides of the argument, *Horace*, like Shakespeare's *Coriolanus*, will doubtless continue to challenge and provoke its audiences to reflection on its sombre illustration of how heroic ideals become entangled in calculations of political advantage and the shifting perspectives of time and changing circumstance. It is surely appropriate then that, like Shakespeare's great Roman tragedy, *Horace* offers no simple answers and instead leads us both to wonder at and to deplore the tragic splendour of a hero whose courage, energy and devotion lead remorselessly to the spectacle of individual hope in ruins.

Notes

1. Founded by Richelieu in 1635 as the literary instrument of a wider centralisation of power. The principal brief of its members was to create a dictionary of French and establish a literary eloquence fit to celebrate the glory of the monarchy.

2. In seventeenth-century France parricide, matricide, fratricide and sororicide were held to be particularly scandalous crimes in so far as they involved the breaking of Natural Law. The term 'parricide' was extended to include any 'unnatural' crime which broke the ties of blood and was commonly used to refer to the killing of a legitimate sovereign, since regicide was an act profoundly destructive of natural relations between humankind and of the natural order governing the body politic.

3. In 1660 Corneille, who had temporarily ceased writing for the stage, published a three-volume collected edition of his plays. Each volume was preceded by a theoretical *Discours*, the first on the moral profit to be gained from dramatic poetry, the second on tragedy, and the third on the unities. This major theoretical treatise took the form partly of a commentary on Aristotle's *Poetics* accompanied by an exposition of his own dramatic principles, and partly of a polemic response to semi-official critical tradition and the Abbé d'Aubignac's *La Pratique du théâtre* of 1657. Furthermore, each play was preceded by an *Examen*, or short critique, of the play's merits and/or deficiencies as they appeared to Corneille in the light of later experience.

4. Robert Brasillach, *Corneille*, Paris, Fayard, 1938.

5. Valdemar Vedel, *Deux Classiques français vus par un critique étranger. Corneille et son temps. Molière*, trans. E. Cornet, Paris, H. Champion, 1935.

6. Louis Herland, 'La Notion de tragique chez Corneille', in *Mélanges de la Société toulousaine d'études classiques*, Toulouse, Privat, 1946, i, pp. 265-84. See also the same author's *Horace ou la naissance de l'homme*, Paris, Editions de Minuit, 1952 (new ed. Toulouse, 1986).

7. Paul Bénichou, *Morales du grand siècle*, Paris, NRF, 1948.

8. Octave Nadal, *Le Sentiment de l'amour dans l'oeuvre de Pierre Corneille*, Paris, Gallimard, 1948 (new ed. Collection TEL, Gallimard, 1991).

9. Jacques Maurens, *La Tragédie sans tragique. Le Néo-stoïcisme dans l'oeuvre de Pierre Corneille*, Paris, Armand Colin, 1966.
André Stegmann, *L'Héroïsme cornélien. Genèse et signification*, 2 vols, Paris, Armand Colin, 1968; see also the later collection of essays by Marc Fumaroli, *Héros et orateurs. Rhétorique et dramaturgie cornéliennes*, Geneva, Droz, 1990.

10. Serge Doubrovsky, *Corneille et la dialectique du héros*, Paris, Gallimard, 1963.

11. D. Trafton, 'On Corneille's *Horace*', *Interpretation*, 2-3 (1972), pp. 183-93 (pp. 192-3).

12. J.-P. Sartre, 'Forgers of Myths', *Theatre Arts*, 30 (1946), pp. 324-35.

HORACE

Characters in order of appearance

SABINA, wife of Horatius and sister of Curiatius
JULIA, a Roman lady, confidante of Sabina and Camilla
CAMILLA, betrothed to Curiatius and sister of Horatius
CURIATIUS, a young Alban nobleman, betrothed to Camilla
HORATIUS, son of Old Horatius
FLAVIAN, an Alban soldier
OLD HORATIUS, a Roman nobleman
VALERIUS, a young Roman nobleman, in love with Camilla
PROCULUS, a Roman soldier
TULLUS, King of Rome

Rome, a room in the house of Horatius.

This translation of *Horace* was commissioned and first presented by Damned Poets Theatre Company at the Lyric Theatre Studio, Hammersmith on 3 October 1996 with the following cast:

SABINA	Louise Bangay
JULIA	Marie Collett
CAMILLA	Esther Hall
CURIATIUS	Alex McSweeney
HORATIUS	Jake Nightingale
FLAVIAN	Ian Regnier-Wilson
OLD HORATIUS	Roger Forbes
VALERIUS	Richard Copestake
TULLUS	Nigel Pegram

Director	Sydnee Blake
Designer	Roy D. Bell
Lighting Designer	David Kidd
Movement Director	Lynn Seymour
Composer	Daniel Biro
Assistant Director	Joy Lo Dico

Co-produced by Diana Maxwell

I.1 Sabina, Julia

SABINA
Don't condemn my weakness . . . Be patient with a grief
That is natural, seeing I have so much to bear.
When a storm like today's is gathering,
The very strongest of us may feel shaken,
And the most manly spirit, the least vulnerable,
Might not keep up its courage without faltering
Although my courage trembles at these events,
The anguish that I feel is not shown by tears.
However much I sigh, and pray to heaven,
I have self-control enough to stop me weeping.   10
When you keep your griefs within bounds like that, it is less
Than a man can achieve – but more than any woman.
To hold back tears in such extremities
Is resolute enough in our own sex.

JULIA
Enough, perhaps, for some ordinary being
Who fears disaster in the smallest danger –
But a brave spirit is ashamed of weakness,
And dares to hope all the more when success is doubtful.
The two camps are pitched down there, below our walls,
And since Rome still doesn't know how to lose a battle,   20
Far from being anxious, you should feel joy for her.
When Rome goes out to fight, she goes to conquer.
Forget, I tell you, forget all your vain fear
And pray with a spirit worthy of a Roman.

SABINA
Yes, I am a Roman, sadly. Horatius is,
And by marrying him I received that title;
But marriage vows would make a chained slave of me
If they cancelled out all thought of where I was born:
Alba, where I first breathed, and saw the light,
Alba, my own dear country, my first love,   30

Now I see you at war with Rome, I dread
Our victory as much as our defeat.
And Rome, if you condemn that as a treason,
Choose for enemies those I can truly hate.
When I see the two armies below your walls, my three
Brothers in one, my husband in the other,
Can I find words without blasphemy to pray
To heaven and beg a victory for you?
I know that your State, still in its infancy,
Cannot add to its power without making war.　　40
I know that it must grow, that your destiny
Extends your bounds beyond the Latin peoples;
I know the gods promise you will rule the world,
And that war alone can bring you such an empire:
Far from opposing this noble fervour,
Which comes of the gods' own plan to make you great,
I want to see your legions, crowned with glory,
Striding in triumph over the Pyrenees,
Launching battalions into Eastern lands,
Setting up Roman standards along the Rhine,　　50
Shaking the very Pillars of Hercules –
But please respect Alba, where your Romulus
Himself was born! From the blood of Alba's kings,
Ungrateful Rome, you derived your name, your walls,
And your first laws. Alba gave birth to you:
Pause and think, now will you strike at your mother's breast?
Can you not carry your triumphant arms
Elsewhere? Alba's joy will salute her children
In their success, she will pray with a mother's love
For Rome – if Rome no longer fights her .　　60

JULIA

What you say shocks me. From the moment we first armed
Our Roman warriors against your country,
I thought you were as indifferent towards Alba
As if you had been one of our Roman race.
I admired the fine strength of mind you showed
When you put your husband's interests before your own.
I sympathised with you in the distress you felt,
As if Rome alone were the cause of all your fears.

SABINA

As long as there were only skirmishes,
Nothing serious enough to bring down either side,   70
And while there were hopes of peace to reassure me –
Yes, I could feel pride in being a Roman.
If I found myself secretly regretful
When Rome rejoiced, at once I checked that impulse.
If I felt any treacherous delight
For my brothers' sake when fate deserted Rome,
To suppress that, I recalled my place, and wept
When glory settled on my brothers' house
But today, when one or other of them must lose,
When Alba is enslaved or Rome defeated,   80
When the outcome of this battle can only mean
No obstacles for the victors and no hope left
For the vanquished, I should have to hate my country
If I still saw myself as wholly Roman,
If I prayed to the gods for a Roman triumph
At the price of so much blood so dear to me.
I cannot give my loyalty to one man.
I am not on Alba's side – I am not on Rome's.
On this decisive day I fear for both,
And will suffer with whoever fate destroys.   90
I shall stay wholly neutral until one wins,
Then take the grief on myself and share no glory.
In the midst of the slaughter, I shall keep
My tears for the vanquished, my hatred for the victors.

JULIA

Is it not curious how often people
Respond in contrasting ways to the same misfortune!
Camilla's reaction is quite unlike your own.
Her brother is your husband, yours her fiancé,
But hers is such a different view from yours –
Of her blood pledged to one force, her love to the
        other.   100
While you gave your whole spirit up to Rome,
Her own – her own faltering spirit – remained unsure.
She feared the worst in each small incident,
Cursed any advantages won by either side,

Wept for the fortunes of whoever lost,
And so she nourished a perpetual grief.
– But yesterday, when she heard today was fixed
For the final battle to be joined at last,
Her face was suddenly radiant with joy –

SABINA
Oh that frightens me, Julia, that she should change so
  quickly,   110
And yesterday she was all smiles with Valerius!
– She has given up Curiatius for this rival.
Are there so many attractions close at hand
That she no longer loves the one she hasn't seen
These last two years? Forgive a sister's love –
I fear for him, and I fear the worst in her.
I find it all too easy to be suspicious:
On such a fateful day you don't change your mind –
Our souls are rarely wounded with some new love
In a crisis like this. One has other thoughts, 120
And I do not think we ought to be exchanging
Sweet pleasantries, and showing such happiness.

JULIA
I find her mood mysterious, just as you do.
I cannot really guess what she is about.
It is firmness enough, at a time of such great danger,
To wait and see – and not to be too frightened.
It is going too far to show any kind of joy.

SABINA
But see – a kind spirit has thought to send her here!
You must try and talk to her about this question,
She is too fond of you to hide her feelings. 130
I'll leave you alone . . . Sister – speak to Julia.
I feel too ashamed to let you see my distress.
My heart is overwhelmed by a thousand griefs,
And I need to hide its pain in solitude.

I.2 Camilla, Julia

CAMILLA

She is quite wrong to want me to talk to you –
Does she think that my grief is any less than hers?
That I am hardened against such misfortunes,
And need to weep less when I speak of them?
My soul is terrified by the same fears.
Like her, I lose whichever army loses.   140
I shall watch my lover, my most precious one,
Die for his country or destroy my own.
He that I love so deeply will require,
In all my grief, that I either mourn or hate him.

JULIA

She has more need of pity than yourself.
One may change a lover, but not a husband.
Forget Curiatius – take your Roman lover,
Then you need not fear at all for the other side.
You will be ours entirely, your soul at peace
With nothing to lose in the camp of our enemies.   150

CAMILLA

You should offer me more honourable advice,
And comfort me without tempting me to crimes.
Although I can barely endure all my afflictions,
I had rather suffer them than deserve them.

JULIA

Is changing your mind with good reason called a crime?

CAMILLA

Is there ever a good reason to break a promise?

JULIA

What is a promise made to an enemy?

CAMILLA

A promise to be kept, like any other.

JULIA

You can't deny it, it's too obvious.
I saw you last night with Valerius again,   160
And that smiling welcome he received from you
Gave him excellent reason to feel hopeful.

CAMILLA

If I talked and smiled with Valerius yesterday,
Don't imagine that I thought to encourage him.
The happiness in my smile was for someone else!
– Hear the truth, so you make no more mistakes;
My love for Curiatius remains too pure
For me to be thought unfaithful one second more.
You remember that Curiatius's sister
Was no sooner joined in marriage to my brother   170
Than Curiatius, completing our happiness,
Gained my father's consent to pledge himself to me?
– That day was both kind and deadly. It united
Our families just as our kings became enemies,
It sealed our betrothal and it brought us war.
Our hope was shattered as soon as it was born,
All that it promised us instantly destroyed,
Making us lovers – and enemies as well.
How many grievous sorrows have followed that,
How many times Curiatius has cursed the gods –   180
And how many rivers of tears run down my cheeks!
I shall say no more. You witnessed our farewells,
And have seen my soul in anguish ever since.
You know what passionate prayers I made for peace,
What tears I wept with each turn of events,
Now for my country, now for my beloved.
In despair at meeting such cruel barriers,
I went to consult the voice of the oracle.
Listen to what it told me yesterday,
And judge if it can help me in my confusion: 190
That famous Greek at the foot of the Aventine hill
Who for many years has foretold people's destinies,
And whom Apollo allows to speak no falsehood,
Prophesied, with these words, that my grief would end:
'Your prayers are answered. The gods have ordained

Peace for Rome and Alba with tomorrow's sun.
You and Curiatius shall from all unkind
Fortune be freed, and eternally made one.'
– I had the fullest faith in this oracle,
And because it offered more than I dared to hope,   200
I abandoned my grieving soul to ecstasies
Far greater than the happiest lovers know.
Do you think I go too far? When I met Valerius,
For once he wasn't merely tiresome to me.
When he spoke of love it wasn't just tedious,
It wasn't like talking to *him* at all.
I couldn't show him the old scorn and coldness –
I was seeing Curiatius, Curiatius everywhere!
Every word I heard affirmed Curiatius's love,
And I pledged my love to him with each word I spoke.   210
Today the armies meet in the final battle.
I heard yesterday, but barely took it in,
My spirit simply refused to contemplate it,
I could only think of marriage, and lasting peace.
– Then last night shattered all my fond illusions:
A thousand evil dreams – vile images –
Huge mountains of dead, scenes of carnage and horror –
Snatched my joy away and brought back my fears.
I saw blood, and corpses, nothing made any sense,
A ghost would appear, and just as quickly vanish;   220
Each scene merged into the next, each dreadful image
Redoubled my fear with its confusion.

JULIA
You need to give a dream an opposite meaning.

CAMILLA
I need to believe that – it's what I long for,
But I find myself now, despite my deepest longings,
Facing a day of battle and not of peace.

JULIA
But it will end the war, and peace will follow.

CAMILLA

If war is the remedy, then let our sufferings
Go on for ever, whether Rome or Alba falls.
Don't long, my love, for the day you will be my
    husband: 230
Never, never will any man be called that
Who either conquers Rome or becomes Rome's slave.
– But what new face do I see here – in this place?
Is it you – *Curiatius*? Do I really see you here?

I.3 Curiatius, Camilla, Julia

CURIATIUS

Yes, you see me, Camilla. And you see a man
Who is neither Rome's conqueror nor its slave.
You need not fear ever seeing these hands stained red
With the shameful weight of chains, or with Roman blood.
I thought you loved Rome and glory well enough
To despise my chains or loathe my victory, 240
And since in this extremity I feared
Conquest and victory almost equally –

CAMILLA

Curiatius – please! – I understand everything.
You have left a war that would shatter all your hopes!
Your heart is mine, and not wanting to lose me,
You deprive your country of your warrior's strength.
Let others worry about your reputation,
And blame you, if they want, for loving me.
Camilla will not think any less of you!
The more you show your love, the more she loves you, 250
And since you owe so much to your native land,
The more you part with, the more you show your love.
– But have you seen my father? Have you his permission
To enter his house as boldly as you do?
Does not the State mean more than family to him,
Does not Rome mean more than his own daughter?
Can we truly believe in this happiness?
Did he see you as son-in-law – or enemy?

CURIATIUS

He greeted me as a son, with a tenderness
That showed it gave him a wholehearted pleasure.   260
In no way did he see me as a traitor,
Unfit for the honour of entering his house.
I have not abandoned my country's cause:
I still love my honour while adoring you!
While the war was on, people recognised in me
The patriot as much as the true lover.
I reconciled my love with the cause of Alba,
I longed for you even while I fought for her,
And if I had to take up arms again,
I should fight for her again, and still yearn for you.   270
Yes, despite what I so passionately desire,
If war resumed, I should fight in my country's cause.
It is peace that allows me access to you here –
And peace to which our love owes this good fortune.

CAMILLA

You say – *peace*? Can I believe in miracles?

JULIA

Camilla, have faith at least in your oracle,
And we shall try to learn how it came about
That the very hour of battle produced this peace.

CURIATIUS

You would never have believed it! Already the two
        armies,
Fired with an equal eagerness for combat,   280
Pride in their step and menace in their eyes,
Only waited for the order to advance –
And then our leader stands out in front of them
And requests, from yours, one moment of delay.
In the silence – 'Romans, what is it we are doing?'
He asks. 'What demon makes us fight each other?
Can't we let the light of reason into our minds?
We are your neighbours – our daughters are your wives,
Marriage has brought so many ties between us
That few of our sons are not cousins of Romans.   290

We come of one stock, one people in two cities –
Why do we ruin ourselves in civil wars
Where deaths among the conquered weaken the
      conquerors,
And each great triumph is nourished by our tears?
Our common enemies wait for that moment
When one side has lost and the other is easy prey,
Broken, exhausted – victorious, yes, but now
Without the help it has itself destroyed.
They have rejoiced so long in our dissension
That we should now combine our powers against them,   300
And consign to oblivion these trifling differences
That turn good soldiers into such bad brothers.
So, seeing that an ambition to rule others
Brings our two armies to this field today,
This same ambition, achieved at lesser cost,
Will not divide us, but unite us all.
We will name certain warriors to represent us,
And trust the entire outcome to those champions.
In accordance with what fate decides for them,
The losing side will surrender to the other,   310
With no dishonour for its brave defenders,
Who would then be subjects without becoming slaves –
No shame, no reparations, no impositions,
Except that one city follow the other's flag.
In that way we forge one empire from two cities.'
– It felt as if his words ended all our discords.
Each man there, looking at the opposing ranks,
Saw a brother-in-law, a cousin, an old friend,
Amazed to think that, avid for blood, his hands
Might in ignorance have committed parricide.   320
You could see it on all their faces, the horror
Of battle, the eagerness to choose champions.
– So the offer was accepted, and the longed-for peace
Immediately agreed; on these conditions:
That three from each side would fight, but our generals
Should give themselves time to make a careful choice.
Your leader is in the senate, ours is in his tent.

CAMILLA

The gods have made me happy with these words –

CURIATIUS

They agreed that within two hours, no more,
The fate of our champions should decide our fate,   330
And while we wait for the names, everyone is free:
Rome is in our camp, we are in the Romans'.
There is liberty of access across the lines,
So everyone can search out his old friends –
I was longing to go and find your brothers,
And when I did, we had such a cordial meting
That your father has promised me, for tomorrow,
The great joy of receiving your hand in marriage.
I trust you will obey your father's wish?

CAMILLA

It is a daughter's duty to obey!   340

CURIATIUS

Come with me then, and hear from his own lips
The words that will make my happiness complete.

CAMILLA

I shall follow you, but I'll go and join my brothers,
To hear from them, too, how all our sorrows ended.

JULIA

Yes, go – and I shall kneel before the altar
And render thanks to the gods on your behalf.

II.1 Horatius, Curiatius

CURIATIUS

So Rome has allowed no others to share this honour,
Thinking any other choice would not seem right?
And this proud city sees you and your two brothers
As the warriors she prefers beyond all the rest?   350
With her famous passion for daring more than others,
She asks one family to face all of us?
Seeing everything placed entirely in your hands,
We might think Horatius's sons were the only Romans!
This choice could have crowned three families with glory,
And made each one's name a blessed memory –
Yes, the honour this choice brings to your great house
Could well have immortalised three families!
And since it is here that good fortune, and my love,
Had me give up a sister and gain a wife,   360
The bonds I have, and shall have, with all of you
Encourage me to claim some of that honour.
Except – there is something that restrains my joy,
And mixes apprehension with all my pleasure.
The war has shown your valour in such a light
That I tremble for Alba, and fear she might well lose.
Since you are named by Rome, her defeat seems certain –
By choosing you, fate has decided so.
I see her darkest purposes in this,
And count myself already a Roman subject.   370

HORATIUS

You should not fear for Alba, but pity Rome,
Seeing whom she forgets – and the three she names.
It was a fatal blindness, to have so many
And then to choose as badly as she has.
A thousand others would have been worthier,
Far better than ourselves to support her cause.
But though this combat promises me a grave,
The glory of being chosen fills me with pride.

It swells my heart with manly confidence.
I dare to place great hopes in my small powers,   390
And whatever jealous fate has in store for me,
I shall not count myself one of your subjects.
Rome puts too much faith in me, but my eager soul
Shall live up to Rome's confidence, or die.
If you vow to win or die you are rarely conquered:
A noble despair is always last to die,
And whatever happens, Romans will not be slaves
Until my dying breaths show I am defeated.

CURIATIUS

And this is why I must feel a deep sorrow:
What my country wants is what my friendship dreads.   390
I think of these two extremes – Alba enslaved,
Or victorious at the cost of a dear life;
The outcome she most earnestly desires
Bought only at the price of your dying breath.
What vows can I make? What happiness expect
When I have tears to weep for either side?
When my hopes for either side are equal treason?

HORATIUS

Would you mourn me if I died serving my country?
For a courageous heart, that death is welcome.
The glory that it brings does not call for tears,   400
And if such an end were mine, I should bless fate
If Rome and the State gained something by my death.

CURIATIUS

All the same, you should allow your friends to fear it.
They alone will grieve if you die so nobly:
You earn your glory, they bear the loss of you,
You will be immortal, and they will taste the grief;
All is lost when a loyal friend is lost.
– But here is Flavian bringing me a message.

II.2 Horatius, Curiatius, Flavian

CURIATIUS
Has Alba made its choice of three warriors?

FLAVIAN
I have come to tell you –   410

CURIATIUS
                    Who are they to be?

FLAVIAN
Your brothers and you.

CURIATIUS
                    Who?

FLAVIAN
                              You, and your two brothers.
But why look so sad? Why do you frown like that?
Does this choice displease you?

CURIATIUS
                              No. It surprises me.
I would not have aspired to so great an honour.

FLAVIAN
Shall I tell the leader, who sent me with this order,
That you received it with so little pleasure?
Your lukewarm welcome for it surprises me.

CURIATIUS
No . . . Tell him friendship, family bonds, and love
Shall not stop Curiatius and his brothers
Serving Alba against Horatius and his.

FLAVIAN
Against – ? I see . . . Those few words say it all.   420

CURIATIUS
Leave us, and take that answer back to him.

II.3 Horatius, Curiatius

CURIATIUS
Now let heaven, and hell, and this very earth
Unite in rage and madness to destroy us!
Let every man, god, demon, and fate itself
Prepare to take up arms against us alone.
I defy them all – fate, demons, gods and men –
To put us in a worse agony than this.
Whatever horrors and cruelties they could send
Would be less than the honour they have done us.   430

HORATIUS
The fate that now opens the gates of honour
Shows our constancy the path to a great glory.
It has used its power to devise a twist of fortune
That will put our courage to the greatest test.
It sees we are no ordinary men,
And rewards us with extraordinary destinies!
To fight an enemy for the common good,
Exposing oneself to injuries from strangers –
Any man with simple courage can do that,
Thousands have, thousands more will do the same: 440
To die for one's country is such a worthy act
That multitudes will desire that splendid death.
But to wish, in the public cause, to kill those you love,
To encounter your other self on the battlefield,
To fight against a side whose defenders are
The brother of your wife and a sister's lover,
So that those bonds are broken, and you loyally fight
Against a family you would die to save –
Only we two possess that resolution!
Few men will envy us this great enterprise,   450
Because few have it written in their hearts
That they could dare to seek such eminence.

CURIATIUS

It is true that now our names can never die.
We must cherish this rare opportunity to show
We are examples of the highest valour –
And yet your resolution seems inhuman.
Few, even of the noblest, would rejoice
In taking this road to immortality.
However highly one may rate this glory,
Obscurity is worth more than such renown.   460
Yes, I will dare to claim – you can bear me out –
That I have never been slow to do my duty:
Long friendship, love, and our family alliance –
None of these things has made me hesitate,
And since Alba makes it clear, by choosing so,
That she values me as much as Rome prizes you,
I shall do as much for her as you do for Rome,
With equal courage. And yet, I am still a man.
I see that your honour commands you to shed my blood,
And that mine bids me to strike you in the heart;   470
That the hand I give the sister must kill the brother,
And that I must do all this for my country's sake . . .
I am quite brave enough to fulfil this duty;
But my heart shrinks from it, I recoil in horror,
I pity myself – and feel envious of those
Whose lives this war has already swallowed up.
– Even so, I don't draw back. This sad, cruel honour
Disturbs me, but does not weaken my resolve.
I value it, and I grieve at what it costs me;
If Rome demands a higher kind of valour,   480
Then I thank the gods I was not born a Roman,
And still have something human left in me.

HORATIUS

If you are not a Roman, be worthy of one,
And if you are my equal, try and show it.
The unshakeable resolve of which I boast
Does not mix the least frailty with its strength.
It does not bode well if one is starting out
On a road like this one with a backward look.
Our misfortune, certainly, cannot be measured,

I see it all – but I do not shrink from it.   490
Whoever my country charges me to fight,
I accept that glory blindly and with joy –
Our pride at receiving such commands
Should extinguish any other feeling in us.
The man who, called upon to serve his country,
Stops to brood on something else, will be ill-prepared:
That sacred trust breaks every other bond.
Rome has chosen me to fight, and I obey.
With an eagerness as full and heartfelt as
My vows to the sister, I shall fight the brother.   500
I have no desire to waste further words on this.
You are Alba's choice, and I no longer know you.

CURIATIUS
I still know you, which is why my heart is breaking.
But this brutal courage was quite unknown to me.
It can no more be measured than our misfortune –
I can admire it, but never copy it.

HORATIUS
No, do not force yourself to be courageous,
And since you take a greater delight in sorrow,
Please feel at liberty to indulge such pleasures.
My sister is coming – no doubt to share them with you.   510
I shall go back to your sister and make sure
She always thinks of herself as Horatius's wife –
But shall love you still, even if you end my life,
And in bereavement show a true Roman strength.

II.4 Horatius, Curiatius, Camilla

HORATIUS
Camilla, have you heard how Alba honours
Your lover?

CAMILLA
Then – my destiny has changed!

HORATIUS

Stay loyal to me, and show yourself my sister,
And if I die – and he returns victorious –
Do not receive him as your brother's murderer,
But as a man who did what he was commanded,   520
Served his country well, and knew how to show,
By his great courage, that he was worthy of you:
Go on with your marriage as if I were still alive.
But if this sword of mine cuts short *his* life,
Regard my victory in the selfsame spirit,
And never reproach me with your lover's death.
Let your tears come. I know your heart is heavy,
So drain it of all its weakness, now, with him.
Blame heaven, and earth, and curse your fate – but when
This combat is over, don't think about the dead.   530
(To Curiatius)
You may stay with her for a few moments only –
Then we shall go together where honour calls us.

II.5 *Camilla, Curiatius*

CAMILLA

Will you go, dear heart? Are you proud of this honour
Which you serve at the cost of all our happiness?

CURIATIUS

Whatever I do I see that I must die,
Either of grief or on Horatius's sword.
I go in torment to this exalted task.
What they ask of me – I curse it a thousand times,
I hate this courage that Alba prizes in me.
My passion turns despair to blasphemy,   540
And holds the gods themselves responsible.
I pity both of us – but I must go.

CAMILLA

No, I know you better. You want me to plead with you,
So my power – as your country sees it – sets you free.

You are famous enough for your other deeds,
You have paid to Alba everything you owe,
No one else has fought more bravely in this war –
No other man has left more Roman dead.
There is nothing you need add to your reputation.
Let some other have the chance to build his own.   550

CURIATIUS
Shall I see some other gloriously crowned
With the immortal laurels prepared for me?
Or have my whole nation blame me, declaring
That, if I had fought, it would have won this war?
That the soldier rested while the lover loved,
And that this brave warrior crowned his career with shame?
No, Alba. Having awarded me this honour,
You will win or lose today through me alone.
You have trusted your fate to one who will answer for it,
And live or die without reproach or blame.   560

CAMILLA
You don't want to see that you are betraying me!

CURIATIUS
There is no betrayal in putting my country first.

CAMILLA
But serving it you lose a brother-in-law,
And your sister a husband.

CURIATIUS
                    That is the bitter truth.
The choice Rome and Alba make has taken away
All sweetness from the words 'brother' and 'sister'.

CAMILLA
So you'll come back here and just throw down his body,
Demanding my hand in marriage as your prize?

CURIATIUS
You must not think such things! I am chosen,

And all I can do is love you without hope.   570
If that makes you weep, my dear one –

CAMILLA
                              All I have is weeping!
My callous lover orders me to die,
And when the nuptial torch is lighted for us,
He dashes it down and leads me to the grave.
This pitiless heart is determined on my death,
And proclaims its love while extinguishing my life.

CURIATIUS
What power there is in a woman's loving tears!
Such a weapon makes her beauty overwhelming . . .
My heart almost relents, to see this sadness,
My resolution almost gives way to it.   580
Do not attack my honour with such grief:
I may not save my courage from your weeping –
I feel it faltering – I cannot defend myself –
The more I am your lover the less I am
Curiatius. I am weak from spurning friendship,
How can I overcome both love and pity?
Go now – do not love me! – and do not weep,
Or I shall commit some outrage against your power.
It will be easier to resist your anger,
And – to deserve that – I no longer love you.   590
Take your revenge on a thankless, inconstant man!
– Are you indifferent to insults of this kind?
– I no longer love you, whatever you may feel!
Is there any more to say? We are not betrothed.
– Does this ruthless duty which makes me its victim
Only let me resist you with violence?

CAMILLA
Commit no other violence, and I swear
I shall not hate you, but love you all the more.
I shall cherish you, whether thankless or treacherous,
If you renounce all thought of this fratricide.   600
Why am I Roman? Why are you not Roman?
I would weave your laurels for you with my own hand,

I would encourage you, not dissuade you,
Treat you in all ways as I have my brother.
The prayers that I made today were made in blindness.
I prayed against you when I prayed for him.
– He is here! I dread to see that his wife's love
Will have had no more power with him than mine with you.

II.6 Horatius, Curiatius, Sabina

CURIATIUS

Sabina is with him! Is Camilla not enough
For my heart to bear? Must it be my sister too?   610
Have you let her tears dissolve all your great courage,
And brought her here to me with the same design?

SABINA

No, no, Curiatius – brother – I only return
To embrace you one last time, and to say good-bye.
Your blood is too noble, nothing I contrive
Would shake the firmness of these virtuous hearts.
If this terrible mischance gave either of you,
Brother or husband, any fear at all,
I would disown him. But may I still say one prayer
Worthy of such a husband, such a brother?   620
I wish with one noble blow to cleanse this contest
Of all impiety, and make its honour pure–
Allow it to occur without taint of crime,
By making lawful enemies of you.
I am the single link that joins you both.
When I am no more, you will have no ties between you.
End your alliance now by breaking that bond:
Since your honour requires you to act from hatred,
Buy with my death the right to hate each other.
Alba wants it, and Rome – you should obey them.   630
Let one of you kill me, the other avenge me,
Then your combat would not seem unnatural,
With one, at least, having justice on his side,
Seeking vengeance for a wife or for a sister.

– Unless you think you might soil your splendid glory
If your anger was stirred up by another cause?
Your love for your country forbids all other ties,
But without them, you would have less to give up to it.
You are forced, without hatred, to kill a brother.
Don't delay in your duty any longer: 640
Begin, by shedding his sister's blood!
Begin by stabbing his wife to the heart!
Begin, with Sabina, to deliver up your lives
As a worthy sacrifice to your dear countries.
We are all enemies in this great combat,
You of Rome, you of Alba – myself of both.
Will you spare me, alone, to see a victory
In which, as the proud ornaments of their glory,
They flaunt the wreaths of a brother or a husband
Still warm with the blood that is so dear to me?   650
Can I share out my loyalty between you?
Do the duty of the sister *and* the wife?
Embrace the victor while I mourn the dead?
But my life will be over before this brutal hour,
My death will still come first, whether it comes
At your hands – or my own, if you refuse me.
– So what is stopping you, inhuman hearts?
I could have you take my life in so many ways:
Your swords will not be so busy in this combat
That I could not find a moment to run between them.   660
Refuse me death now, and you will need to strike
Through this body first if you want to wound each other.

HORATIUS

My wife!

CURIATIUS

    My sister!

CAMILLA

        Sabina – they are relenting!

SABINA

Your words – and your faces – tell me everything.

Are you frightened? Are these really the brave hearts
Rome and Alba have chosen for their champions?

HORATIUS

Sabina, what hurt have I ever done you,
What wrong have I done that asks for such revenge?
What harm has my honour done you, that you claim
This right to besiege my courage with such force?   670
Be content with knowing that you have moved me –
But let me go now, to finish this day's great task.
You unsettle me in a way I have never known . . .
Show you love me enough to go no further.
Leave me – don't put our victory in doubt,
This arguing has shamed me enough already.
Allow me to end my days with honour.

SABINA

Go, then. You need not fear me – help is coming.

II.7 Old Horatius, Horatius, Curiatius, Sabina, Camilla

OLD HORATIUS

What is this, my sons? Is this a day for love?
Are you still here, wasting time with women?   680
Will their tears prepare you for shedding blood?
You must leave now, and leave them to their sorrows.
If you are swayed by their artful tenderness,
They will make you as vulnerable as themselves.
You can only avoid that if you go at once.

SABINA

Don't be anxious about them, they are worthy of you.
For all our efforts, you may still expect them
To behave like your true son and son-in-law,
And if our weakness has unsettled them,
We shall leave you here to strengthen their resolve.   690
We will go, Camilla, and waste no more time on tears:

They are weak weapons, against so much honour.
Nothing remains for us beyond despair.
Go and fight, tigers! We shall go and die.

II.8 Old Horatius, Horatius, Curiatius

HORATIUS
Father, keep them here – they cannot control themselves.
I must tell you, if you let them leave this house
Their wilful emotions are bound to lead them on
To interrupt our combat with tears and protests –
Given what they are to us, the world will think
It is some stratagem we have organised.   700
The honour of being chosen would turn sour
If anyone suspected us of cowardice.

OLD HORATIUS
I will take care of that. Your brothers are waiting.
Think nothing beyond what your countries ask of you.

CURIATIUS
How should I take my leave? And what farewell –?

OLD HORATIUS
Do not try. What you say might cause me to give way.
I, too, have no words suited to this moment –
My heart will not allow me to find the thoughts.
All I can say farewell with is . . . these tears.
Do your duty, and let the gods decide.   710

III.1 Sabina

SABINA

In this time of sorrows, I am forced to choose:
To be wife of one, or sister of the other,
No longer sharing out this futile grief,
But making a choice, with that much less to fear.
Yet which to choose, when fate is so perverse?
Is my husband or my brother the enemy?
Love pleads for one, and kinship for the other,
And the law of duty binds me to each of them.
– Then why not emulate their noblest feelings,
Be wife and sister both, at the same time,   720
Accept their honour as the highest good,
Be as strong as they are – and banish all fear?
The death they are facing is so beautiful
That I shall not need to fear as I wait for news.
We shall not speak of pitiless destiny:
We should think of the cause, not the hand that kills for it,
And when we greet the victors, welcome the glory
That such a victory brings back to their house;
And, not considering whose blood was shed
So their courage could raise them up in splendour,   730
Make the victory of that family our own triumph.
In one house I am wife, in the other daughter,
And tied to each by such strong bonds that neither
Can triumph except through the strength of those dear to
      me.
Fortune – whatever sufferings you send me,
I have found a way of turning them into joys!
I can watch today's combat bravely, see the dead
And not despair, see the victors without horror.
. . . All a flattering delusion, an empty dream!
All a fantasy, a feeble shaft of light   740
Which blinded me with an empty brilliance
I knew would never last, and would soon vanish!
Like those lightnings which, through the blackest shadows,

Strike with the light of day, then die and leave
The dark world darker still, it cleared my vision
Only to cast me into deeper night.
It charmed my pain away, heaven is angry
And makes me pay for that moment of relief.
I feel my grieving heart pierced by the blows
Now striking down a brother, or my husband.   750
When I think of their death, however much I try,
I think of the hand that kills, not the noble cause;
And when I see the conquerors in their splendour,
I can only think of whose blood was shed for it.
My heart is with the family of the vanquished:
In one house I am daughter, in the other wife,
And tied to each by such strong bonds that neither
Can triumph except by killing those dear to me.
Is this the peace which I desired so much?
You gods! – you have been kind, and heard me out.   760
What afflictions will you send down in your anger,
If your kindness brings such cruelty with it?
In what way will you punish some real offence
If this rewards the prayers of innocence?

III.2 Sabina, Julia

SABINA
Is it over, Julia? What have you come to tell me?
Am I to mourn a brother – or a husband?
Has the grim success of their inhuman arms
Left not a single combatant alive,
And, refusing me my horror of the victors,
Ensured that I must weep for all of them?   770

JULIA
And so you still know nothing of what has happened?

SABINA
Does it surprise you that I know nothing?
You truly did not know that they made this house

A prison for Camilla and myself?
They confined us here, Julia, frightened of our tears:
We might otherwise have run between their swords,
And in the desperation of our love
Roused at least some pity in the two camps.

JULIA

No such tender demonstration was required,
The sight of who they were was enough for that.   780
The moment they strode out, ready to begin,
A murmur started up in both the armies
On seeing these friends, men so close to each other,
Prepared to kill and die out of national pride.
Some are moved to pity, some are horrified,
Others admire their patriotic zeal
And think they show incomparable spirit.
Some dare to call it brutal, and blasphemous.
But, for all these differences, everyone there
Unites to blame the two kings and curse their choice,   790
And, not prepared to watch so obscene a contest,
They shout out protests, break ranks – and separate them!

SABINA

You gods have heard my prayers, you shall have my
        offerings!

JULIA

Sabina, it is not yet as you imagine.
You may hope a little, and you have less to fear,
But you still have much to make you suffer.
– Trying to save them from their fate proved useless.
These hardened warriors are beyond persuading:
The glory of being chosen is so precious,
And so bewitching to their ambitious spirits,   800
That where we feel sorry for them, they feel exultant,
And regard our pity as a mortal insult.
All these protests stain their reputation,
They would sooner fight both armies by themselves,
And die at the hands of those restraining them,
Than renounce the honour such a choice confers.

SABINA

So they hardened their hearts of steel? – and didn't relent?

JULIA

They did not. But the two camps are in uproar,
And the same shout goes up from either side,
Calling for war unless different men are chosen.   810
The presence of their leaders makes little difference,
They have almost lost control, no one listens to them,
The King himself is shaken . . . With one last effort:
'We are all,' he declares, 'so troubled and divided,
We should ask the great gods for their decision,
And see if a change of plan would accord with it.
No man would dare to defy their sacred will
As revealed to us through a holy sacrifice.'
When he finished, it seemed his words had worked
        a spell
To prise the swords out of even those warriors' hands.   820
Despite that lust for glory which blinds their eyes
To anything else, they still revere the gods,
So their angry spirit yields to the King's advice –
And whether from deference, or some sudden scruple,
Both armies agree to be ruled by it
As if each side regards Tullus as its king.
We shall learn the rest when the ritual beasts are
        slaughtered.

SABINA

The gods will not allow such a monstrous combat.
Now it is postponed, my hopes are high,
And I begin to see my prayers are granted.   830

III.3 Sabina, Camilla, Julia

SABINA

Camilla! – Let me tell you some good news –

CAMILLA

I think I know – if you can call it good . . .

They came to tell my father, I was with him;
But I found nothing in it to calm my fears.
Delaying our sufferings only makes them harsher,
And merely prolongs all our anxiety.
The only relief we can hope to gain from this
Comes from mourning later those we are forced to mourn.

SABINA

The gods did not inspire that revolt in vain.

CAMILLA

It is truer to say that we consult them in vain.   840
The same gods inspired Tullus to choose those warriors,
And the people's voice is not always the gods' voice.
The gods speak much less often through humble mouths
Than they do through their living images, our kings,
Whose holy and independent power is like
A secret ray of light they receive from heaven.

JULIA

You are seeking to find something harsher for yourself
If you try to look beyond their oracles –
And you cannot believe that everything is lost
Without denying what you heard yesterday.   850

CAMILLA

But an oracle never allows of understanding.
You always grasp less than you think you grasp,
And if you take any comfort from its verdict,
You have stared into darkness and imagined light.

SABINA

We should feel reassured by what has happened,
And allow ourselves some just and pleasant hope.
When heaven offers a little kindness to us,
Those who expect no favour will not deserve it –
They will often prevent heaven from granting it,
Or lose it by their refusal when it comes.   860

CAMILLA

Heaven acts despite us in all these matters,
And takes no account at all of personal feelings.

JULIA

It only frightened you to show you mercy.
Good-bye: I shall go to find out what has happened.
Try not to be afraid. When I return,
I hope we shall need only to speak of love –
And that we see out this day's final hours
With preparations for a happy wedding.

SABINA

I still dare to hope for that.

CAMILLA

                           I hope for nothing.

JULIA

Events will prove to you that we were right.   870

III.4 Sabina, Camilla

SABINA

This is a time of grief, but I must be frank:
I cannot sympathise with all your sorrow.
What would you do, dear sister, in my place,
With as much to fear as I have to fear myself –
And if you saw this fatal conflict ending
With losses and misfortunes as great as mine?

CAMILLA

Speak more thoughtfully of your and my sufferings.
We don't see another's pain as we do our own,
But if you could sense what heaven inflicts on me,
Your grief would seem no worse than an evil dream.   880
You need only to fear Horatius's death.
Our brothers count for little beside a husband:

Marriage, which joins you to a new family,
Breaks all ties with the one where you were a daughter,
And you see such different bonds with other eyes
Since you left your parents for a husband's sake.
But, close to my wedding, my loved one, his father's gift,
Is less than a husband to me, and like a brother –
And my feelings therefore waver between the two,
My choice impossible and my prayers confused.   890
At least, dear sister, your sorrows offer you
One clear thing to hope for that ends your fears.
But if heaven persists in its persecutions,
I have everything to fear, and no hope at all.

SABINA

But as one of these two must die – at the other's hand –
I am in a situation far worse than yours.
Although the ties are wholly different,
You do not forget your parents when you leave them.
Marriage does not efface those influences –
To love a husband you need not hate your brothers.   900
Your bonds with them retain their early strength,
And no choice you make should ever cost their lives.
They – like a husband – are our other selves,
And all deep griefs have the same intensity.
But the lover who enthrals you, and stirs your passion,
Is only, in the end, what you make of him.
Ill-temper, or some trace of jealousy,
Often blows away a dream of ideal love.
Caprice can do that – let reason do it now;
Allow your family ties to be paramount.   910
It is a crime to set up your chosen bonds
Against all those deriving from your birth.
If heaven goes on persecuting us,
I have everything to fear, nothing to hope for.
As for you, you will suffer – but duty says
You may hope for something yet, and end your fears.

CAMILLA

I see it all, my sister. You have never loved,
You know nothing at all of love and how it wounds.

We might resist it at the very start:
We cannot banish it when it is our master,   920
And when a father's pledge has sealed our bond,
Then this tyrant is made a lawful king.
Love arrives so gently, but it rules by force,
And once the soul has yielded to its power,
It becomes impossible for you not to love.
You can only ever do what love decrees –
Its bonds are as strong as they are beautiful.

III.5 Old Horatius, Sabina, Camilla

OLD HORATIUS
Daughters – I come to bring you grievous news.
I could not have tried to conceal from you
What would not have been hidden for very long –   930
Your brothers are fighting; it was the gods' command.

SABINA
I am horrified . . . There is nothing I can say . . .
So I deceived myself when I assumed
The gods were not unjust, but merciful!
No! – don't console us. Pity pleads in vain
Against such misfortune, and reasoning sounds empty.
We could end all our griefs with our own hands,
And those who die that way can defy all pain;
We could easily contrive, in your presence,
To hide our despair in a show of self-control –   940
But when we can show weakness without shame,
It would seem quite disgraceful to pretend.
Shall we leave that hypocrisy to men,
Preferring to be seen as we truly are?
We do not ask of you that your great courage
Should follow our own example, and curse fate.
You should take this appalling news without trembling,
Witness our tears – but do not weep yourself,
And then, for your dignity's sake, even through such
        torments,

Preserve your peace of mind and bear with our grief.   950

OLD HORATIUS

Far from blaming you for the tears I see you weep,
I must confess I can scarcely hold back my own.
If I needed to endure as much as you,
I might easily give in to such brutal blows.
Alba has chosen, and still I can't hate your brothers,
All three of them are still most dear to me –
But in the end, friendship is not the same
As love or kinship, its influence is weaker.
I don't feel the same anguish that torments
Sabina as a sister, or Camilla   960
As a lover. Those men are my enemies,
And I have no qualms about siding with my own sons.
I thank the gods they are worthy of their country;
They have not flinched and soiled their reputation.
I saw their honour double instantly
When they refused the pity of the two camps.
If they had been so weak as to plead for it,
If they had not rejected it so nobly,
I would have found revenge with my own sword
For the shame their cowardice would have brought
        on me.   970
Yet when, all the same, they wanted to choose others,
I can't pretend! – I prayed then as hard as you.
If heaven had been merciful, and heard me,
Then Alba would have had to choose differently.
We should have seen Horatius and his brothers
Victorious without spilling Curiatius' blood.
We should have been praising Roman honour now
At the outcome of a more humane encounter.
But the gods in their wisdom decided otherwise,
And my spirit must accept their eternal will.   980
At this terrible hour it finds strength in selflessness,
And happiness in serving the public cause.
Try to do so yourselves, to relieve your sorrows,
Remembering – both of you – that you are Romans.
You *(to Sabina)* have become one – and you *(to Camilla)* are
        still a Roman.

Such a glorious title is a special jewel:
A day will come, a day in the future when
All the earth fears Rome as it fears the heavens' thunder,
When the universe trembles under Roman rule,
And kings aspire to the very name of 'Roman' –   990
Such is the glory the gods promised Aeneas.

III.6 Old Horatius, Sabina, Camilla, Julia

OLD HORATIUS
You come to bring the news of victory?

JULIA
To say that what you dreaded most has happened!
Rome has fallen to Alba, your sons are routed,
Of the three, two are dead – and only her husband lives.

OLD HORATIUS
No outcome could be more truly terrible!
Rome has fallen to Alba, and Horatius
Did not fight to protect her until his final breath?
This cannot be so, they are deceiving you.
Rome would not fall before Horatius died.   1000
I know my blood – it understands its duty.

JULIA
I, and thousands, saw it all, from the battlements,
And applauded his efforts while his brothers lived –
But when he saw he was one against three opponents
And almost surrounded, he ran back to save his life.

OLD HORATIUS
He betrayed our soldiers and they did not kill him?
They let this coward hide in their ranks for safety?

JULIA
I wanted to see no more after this defeat.

CAMILLA

Then my brothers – !

OLD HORATIUS

Don't try to speak, or weep for them.
The two of them share a fate their father envies.   1010
Let their graves be covered with the finest flowers;
The glory of their death repays my loss.
Their unconquerable hearts knew the happiness
Of seeing Rome free as long as they were alive,
Rome subject to none but her rightful king
And not made the province of any neighbour state.
But weep for the third, and the mark of slavery
Burned on our foreheads by his shameful flight;
Weep for the dishonour of all our race,
And the eternal slur on the name of Horatius.   1020

JULIA

What should one have done against three?

OLD HORATIUS

Died, for Rome!
Or found some final courage in despair.
Had he held off defeat one moment more,
Rome would have been enslaved just that much later,
He would have saved some honour for my last years,
And could worthily have paid his life for that.
All the blood he has he owes to his country –
Each drop he denied it stains his reputation.
Each future minute of his craven life
Adds to my own disgrace as it adds to his.   1030
I shall use my rights against an unworthy son
And end his life at once, so my just anger
Will announce to the world, in punishing him thus,
My immeasurable contempt for what he has done.

SABINA

Do not think so much of your anger, and your rights –
It will only serve to deepen our misery.

OLD HORATIUS

You are too easily comforted, Sabina.
So far our misfortunes have barely touched you.
You still have no share in our profound distress:
Heaven has saved your husband and your brothers,   1040
And if we are subjects, your Alba is our master;
Your brothers are victorious while Rome is betrayed,
And, seeing the high point Alba's glory reaches,
You cannot appreciate our sense of shame –
Though your excessive love for such a husband
Will soon give you ample cause to mourn like us!
Your tears for him won't protect him against me:
I call the vast powers of the gods to witness
That before this day is out, these very hands
Will cleanse Rome of its shame with Horatius's blood!   1050
                                              (Exit)

SABINA

Quickly! – We must go with him – he is crazed with anger.
You gods! – is it always our destiny to suffer?
Must we always expect yet worse disasters?
Always to go in fear of our loved ones' swords?

IV.1 Old Horatius, Camilla

OLD HORATIUS

Don't plead with me for this traitor. He ran away
From his wife's three brothers, let him run from me!
He will have no way of saving his precious life
Unless he stays out of my sight. Sabina
Shall not protect him – or I shall again
Call to witness the power of all the gods in heaven . . .   1060

CAMILLA

Father! Will you not be more forgiving?
You will see that Rome itself thinks otherwise,
And, whatever misfortune heaven called down on him,
Will excuse him the duty of courage when so outnumbered.

OLD HORATIUS

To me Rome's opinion is of small importance.
I am his father and therefore have my rights.
I know too well what genuine courage means:
Overwhelmed, it still finds triumph in defeat –
Though manly strength may succumb to greater numbers,
It fights without fear until the very last.   1070
Quiet now! – Let us hear what Valerius wants with us.

IV.2 Old Horatius, Valerius, Camilla

VALERIUS

The King sends me to offer to a father
Deepest sympathies –

OLD HORATIUS

Save yourself the effort!
I have no need of any such consolation.
The two sons I lost to our enemy today

Are better dead than surviving in disgrace.
They died like men of honour, for their country.
I could wish no more.

VALERIUS
But the third son brought you joy.
Your surviving son can stand for all three of them.

OLD HORATIUS
I wish the name Horatius had died with him.   1080

VALERIUS
Only you speak so harshly, after what he did.

OLD HORATIUS
And only I can punish him for his crime.

VALERIUS
How can you call his bold resource a crime?

OLD HORATIUS
What credit is there in running for his life?

VALERIUS
But on this occasion flight proved glorious.

OLD HORATIUS
You redouble my shame and my confusion!
It would seem truly rare and memorable
If a coward had run away in pursuit of glory.

VALERIUS
What shame, and what confusion, should you feel
At fathering a son who has saved us all?   1090
Who has given Rome a victory – and a conquest?
What greater honours would a father want?

OLD HORATIUS
How can you speak of honour – victory – conquest,
When the laws of Alba must decide our future?

VALERIUS

How can you speak as if Alba had triumphed?
Are you aware of only half the story?

OLD HORATIUS

I know that my son fled – and betrayed his country.

VALERIUS

If the combat had ended there, that might be true.
But we all soon realised that was a stratagem
For turning the day to Rome's advantage.   1100

OLD HORATIUS

Are you saying – *Rome* triumphed?

VALERIUS

                                      You knew nothing about
The courage of this son whom you are maligning?
– He is one against three, but he has no injuries,
Whereas all of his opponents have suffered wounds.
He is too weak to take on three – though stronger than
        each –
And he sees how he can escape a mortal danger.
Yes, he runs away – but this is a clever ruse
To divide those three, and fight to better purpose.
Each is equally eager to overhaul him,
And chases him – at a lesser or greater speed   1110
According to the severity of his wounds –
But they are separated by that difference.
Horatius looks round – and sees they are far apart –
He turns – and knows they are already beaten!
He waits for the first, your intended son-in-law –
Who is furious that Horatius dares just to stand there,
And engages with him. But even his great heart
Is weakened by the loss of so much blood.
Alba dreads to think that fate has now changed sides,
And their soldiers call to the second to help his
        brother.   1120
That one hurries to join him – but his efforts exhaust him,
And he gets there only to find his brother dead.

CAMILLA

His – ?

VALERIUS

Gasping for breath, he takes his brother's place –
And soon Horatius has another victim:
The man is too weak, his courage is not enough,
He falls beside the one he hoped to avenge.
The air is loud with the cries of both the armies,
Alba's in anguish and the Romans' in sheer joy.
Now our brave warrior sees it is almost over,
But this is not enough, he shouts a challenge: 1130
'I have sacrificed these two to my brothers' spirits.
Rome itself shall have the last of my three rivals:
He shall be a sacrifice for my country.'
And at once, as we all watch, he flies at him –
And no one doubts what the end of this will be.
The wounded man can barely lift his sword,
And, like a victim at some holy altar,
Seems to offer his throat for the mortal blow,
Receiving it with virtually no defence –
And with his death Rome's empire is established!   1140

OLD HORATIUS

O my son! O pride of all our days!
O unlooked-for saviour of a land in danger!
True child of Rome – and of Horatius's house!
Hero of your country, glory of your race!
When can I embrace you, and wipe out the wrong
I did to you by forming such false opinions?
When can my love for you, in its great tenderness,
Bathe your hero's brow in tears of happiness?

VALERIUS

You will be able to embrace him soon:
The King is about to send him back to you.   1150
He postpones until tomorrow the ceremony
Of sacrifice to the gods for our deliverance.
Today we shall simply give our thanks to them
In songs of victory and heartfelt prayers.

The King is praying now, and in the meantime
Sends me, with these words of sympathy and joy.
But messages alone are not enough:
He will come here himself, perhaps even today,
Believing such valour has not been recognised
Unless you can hear his praise from his own lips,   1160
In your own house, and be told of Rome's debt to you.

OLD HORATIUS

Such personal thanks would honour me too highly.
I am well paid already by your own words,
For one son's service and two sons' glorious deaths.

VALERIUS

The King does not know how to honour men by halves,
And with his sceptre snatched out of enemy hands,
He considers the honour he bestows on you
Still insufficient for both the son and father.
I shall go and bear witness to the noble thoughts
Inspired in you by your courage on this day –   1170
And tell him, too, of your fervour in his cause.

OLD HORATIUS

I am deeply in your debt for such a kindness.

IV.3 Old Horatius, Camilla

OLD HORATIUS

My daughter – this is no time for shedding tears.
It is wrong to weep when we have gained such honours,
And quite out of place to mourn our own misfortunes
When they have brought a victory for the State.
Rome has conquered Alba! – that is enough.
Our losses are a price we should gladly pay.
In your lover's death, you have lost only a man –
Rome can easily replace him with another,   1180
And besides, after this victory, no Roman
Would not feel proud to offer you his hand.

I must go and tell Sabina about this news.
It can only be a grievous blow for her,
And with three brothers dead by a husband's hand,
She will have much greater reason than you to weep.
– I hope I can prevent any storm of tears.
A little common-sense and her great courage
Should soon ensure that her noble heart is ruled
By the love she owes the victor as her husband.   1190
You, meanwhile, should forget your own shameful grief.
Meet Horatius, if he comes, with no sign of frailty.
Show him you are his sister, shaped by heaven
In the same womb, and with the same Roman blood.

IV.4 Camilla

CAMILLA

Yes, I will make him see, beyond any doubt,
That a true love defies the scheming of the Fates
And will not obey the laws of these cruel tyrants
Given us as parents by a malicious star.
You condemn my grief? You dare to call it shameful?
I cherish it all the more, pitiless father,   1200
The more it offends you; and I am entitled
To wish the offence were as great as my suffering.
Was there ever anyone whose evil fortune
Took so many different forms in so short a time,
Changing from sweet to bitter in one minute,
Inflicting so much before the final blow?
Was there ever a heart so visited in a day
By joy and sorrow, hope and abject fear,
So forced to be the slave of mere event,
The pitiable toy of circumstance?   1210
An oracle comforts me – then nightmare torments me.
Peace calms my terror at the thought of battle,
And my wedding is arranged – then instantly
Curiatius is chosen to challenge my own brother.
I am in despair – but they all refuse that choice,
So the plan is dropped. Yet the gods insist on it.

Rome seems conquered – and alone of the three Albans
Curiatius is not stained with my family's blood.
Do the gods chastise me, for feeling so little grief
At Rome's defeat and my two brothers' death?   1220
Did I expect too much when I dared to think
I might, without treachery, love him and have some hope?
I am well punished by his death, and the cruel way
In which my distracted mind has to bear the news:
His rival tells me, insisting that I see
All the hideous details of his victory . . .
As he speaks, he can't conceal his own delight,
Less at the triumph than at what I suffer,
Building false hopes on someone else's death
And gloating over him, as my brother did.   1230
But this is nothing to what follows now:
I am required to be joyful on this dark day,
I have to applaud the conqueror's achievements,
And kiss the hand that stabs me to the heart!
I have the right to weep, but I am told
Weeping is shameful, sorrow is a crime.
Their brutal virtue demands that we be joyful,
If we show human feelings, we are cowards.
– I shall renounce my father's callous virtue,
And be an unworthy sister to this brave brother.   1240
There is glory in being held contemptible
When brutality is turned into a virtue.
I shall weep. What good can come of holding back?
What is left to fear when you lose everything?
For this heartless conqueror I shall show no respect;
In no way avoid him, but face up to him,
Denounce his victory and rouse his fury,
– And take my pleasure from offending him.
He is coming now! – I shall have him learn from me
What a woman owes to her lover's memory.   1250

IV.5 Horatius, Camilla, Proculus

(Proculus carries in his hand the swords of the three Curiatii)

HORATIUS

Sister, this hand avenged our two dead brothers,
And changed our hostile destinies to make us
Masters of Alba. This hand by itself, today,
Decided the fate of our two nations.
These trophies are the symbols of my glory –
Give them the honour due to victory!

CAMILLA

You may have my tears – I owe victory nothing else.

HORATIUS

Rome does not look for tears after such achievement,
And our two dead brothers, fallen in the war,
Were too well avenged to need any weeping.   1260
When deaths like theirs are avenged, you have lost nothing.

CAMILLA

Because they are atoned for by the blood spilt,
I shall not show any further grief for them.
You have avenged their deaths – I shall forget them.
But who will avenge me for my lover's death,
And allow me to forget it in one instant?

HORATIUS

What, exactly, do you mean?

CAMILLA

                    My dear one! – Curiatius!

HORATIUS

Has my unworthy sister the insolence,
The unspeakable audacity, to name
The enemy I conquered as her 'dear one'?   1270
That is a treachery, and it asks for vengeance:

Your words require it, and your heart longs for it.
Control your shameful passions and desires,
Don't have me blush to hear your cries of sorrow.
From now on you must not permit these passions
To burn inside you. Banish them! – think and speak
Only of these, my spoils of victory.

CAMILLA

Then – barbarian! – give me a heart like yours.
Do you really wish to hear my most secret thoughts?
– I want Curiatius back! – or let me mourn!   1280
All my joy and grief hung on his fortunes.
I loved him living – and I mourn him dead.
You must never look for the sister you once knew –
All you will see in me is the stricken lover,
Who will follow your every movement like a fury,
And never let you forget Curiatius's death.
Bloodthirsty tiger, you deny me tears,
You ask me to rejoice in my dear one's death,
And praise your fine achievements to high heaven –
So that I kill him myself, a second time?   1290
May your life be so full of cruel misfortunes
That in the end you find you are envying me,
And staining with some dishonourable act
The glory now so dear to your brutal heart!

HORATIUS

I call upon the gods to witness this!
Do you think I can suffer you to insult me?
Endure this mortal slur on our noble house?
You shall rejoice, rejoice in the death that saved us,
And devote yourself not to one man's memory
But to the good of Rome, which gave you birth.   1300

CAMILLA

Rome, the one cause of all my bitterness!
Rome, for whose sake you sacrificed my love!
Rome which you worship, and which saw you born!
Rome which I hate because she honours you.
May all Rome's neighbouring countries join together

To sap her foundations while there is still time,
And if all of Italy proves not enough for that,
May East and West together combine against her,
May a hundred powers from all corners of the earth
Reach across seas and mountains to destroy her,   1310
May Rome pull down her own walls upon herself,
And tear herself apart with her own hands!
May heaven's anger, kindled by my prayers,
Send down a rain of liquid fire on Rome!
May I live to see this carnage with my own eyes,
See houses burn and laurels char to ash,
And the last man in Rome die aware that I alone
Brought this about – then may I die, of joy!

HORATIUS
(laying his hand on his sword and rushing after
her as she runs out)
I have listened patiently – now reason shall speak.
You shall mourn Curiatius in the depths of hell!   1320

CAMILLA
(wounded, offstage)
You betray your own blood –!

HORATIUS
(returning)
                              This punishment falls at once
On whoever dares to mourn Rome's enemies!

IV.6 Horatius, Proculus

PROCULUS
What is it you have done – ?

HORATIUS
                              An act of justice.
Her treason deserved immediate retribution.

PROCULUS
But surely not such ruthlessness –

HORATIUS
                                        Don't tell me
That she was of our blood, and was my sister.
My father will not see her as his daughter.
In cursing Rome, she disowned her family,
And forfeits her right to either beloved name.
Her closest kinsmen became her enemies,   1330
And their common blood makes them hate her all the
      more.
My immediate vengeance was entirely just:
Although her impious curses had no power,
It was best to choke the monster at its birth.

IV.7 Horatius, Sabina, Proculus

SABINA
Why should you let your noble rage stop there?
Come and watch your sister die in your father's arms,
Feast your courage on that sweet and glorious sight –
Or if you have strength for further acts of justice,
Offer up to your dear country, Horatius's Rome,
This last sad remnant of Curiatius's race.   1340
You have shed blood of your own, you need not spare
      theirs:
Add Sabina to Camilla, sister and wife.
Our treasons and our sorrows are the same,
I weep like her, I mourn for my three brothers,
And I am more guilty of breaking your cruel laws:
She weeps for only one, I weep for three,
She is punished, I persist in the same crime.

HORATIUS
Sabina, dry your tears, or hide them from me.
Be worthy of the name of Horatius's wife –
Don't try to stir me to unworthy pity.   1350

If all the sovereign power of our pure love
Does not mean that in mind and soul we are the same,
You must raise your feelings to my higher plane,
Not require that I descend to the shame of yours.
I love you, and I understand your grief:
You should draw on my strength to overcome your
    weakness,
Share in my glory, and not tarnish it,
Wear it yourself, not seek to strip me of it.
Are you such a mortal enemy of my honour
That I would please you more if I were disgraced?   1360
Be the wife, not the sister, be guided by me,
And make my example your unchanging rule.

SABINA

You should look for more perfect people to imitate you.
I do not blame you for my brothers' deaths –
I am bound to feel about them as I do,
And I blame fate, rather than your sense of duty.
But I utterly renounce your Roman 'courage',
If I have to be inhuman to possess it.
I cannot see in myself the conqueror's wife
Without also seeing the sister of those he killed.   1370
In public we can join the celebrations,
But here, in our home, we must mourn for our own dead,
And set aside all thoughts of the public good
When we think of the sorrows that are ours alone.
It is cruel of you to want to do otherwise –
When you enter here, leave your triumphs at the door
And mingle your tears with mine. – So! these shameful
    thoughts
Don't arm your courage to end this wretched life?
Doesn't my further crime stir you to fury?
How happy Camilla is! She made you angry,   1380
She won from you just what she set out to gain,
And all that she lost is given back to her.
Dear husband – dearest cause of all my anguish –
If your anger dies, then listen to your pity;
After all these terrors you may use either,
To chastise my weakness or to end my pain.

I ask for death – in mercy or in torment,
Given from love or justice, no matter which.
What I suffer in dying will be sweet suffering
If I receive it from a husband's hand.   1390

HORATIUS

How unjust the gods are, to grant to women
Such prodigious power over the finest spirits,
Delighting in the sight of their frailty
So easily ruling over the noblest hearts!
– And all my manhood is reduced to this,
That nothing will save it except to run away.
Farewell. Do not follow me – or do not weep.

SABINA
(Alone)

O anger, O pity! Deaf to my desires,
You ignore my crime, and my suffering wearies you.
I have not found either punishment or mercy.   1400
I shall follow him – but if I weep in vain,
I can look to my own courage to end my pain.

V.1 Old Horatius, Horatius

OLD HORATIUS
We shall turn our thoughts away from this grim sight
To consider the judgement of the gods.
When glory boosts our confidence too much,
They know how to humble our presumptuous pride:
They send our sweetest pleasures mixed with sadness,
They mingle blemishes with all our virtues,
And they will rarely grant to our ambition
That it be wholly honourable and pure.   1410
I do not pity Camilla – hers was a crime!
I am more to be pitied, and I pity you more than her,
Myself for fathering a treacherous daughter,
And you that you stained your hands by killing her.
I find nothing wrong or impulsive in your deed,
But you should have saved yourself the stigma of it.
Her crime, though deserving death, was better left
Unpunished than punished by a brother's hand.

HORATIUS
The laws give you all power over my life;
I knew her blood belonged to my place of birth.   1420
If, in your view, my fervour is a crime,
If I must carry it like a scar, for ever,
If this hand of mine is degraded and profaned,
You may take this life away with a single word,
You may take this blood, whose purity
Is tainted for ever by my infamy.
I could not allow her treason in your race –
You should not suffer my stain on our ancient house.
In such instances, where honour is compromised,
A father like yourself has to intervene: 1430
His love should be silent where there is no excuse,
And if he conceals a crime, he involves himself.
He gives too little thought to his own reputation
If he condemns the crime and will not punish.

OLD HORATIUS

This father is not always so merciless.
He often spares his own sons for his own sake,
He would wish them to support him in old age,
And knows that his punishments would harm himself.
My view of you is quite different from your own.
I know – But the King comes! These are his officers.   1440

V.2 Tullus, Valerius, Old Horatius, Horatius, guards

OLD HORATIUS

Sir, you honour me too much by coming here.
This is hardly where I should think to meet my king:
Let me, on my knees –

TULLUS

Sir, I ask you not to kneel!
I do only what a monarch needs to do.
Such rare devotion – such decisive skill –
Deserve some rare and special recognition.
(Indicating Valerius)
You have had his word, already, as a pledge.
And I did not wish to postpone it any longer.
He told me – though I never doubted it –
How calmly you faced up to your two sons' deaths.   1450
I know that after even so short a time
Your courageous heart will not need my consolation.
– But I have just learned of this strange tragedy
That followed the triumph of your brave third son:
How his fierce patriotism led him on
To lay violent hands on his father's only daughter.
A loss like that would shake the strongest spirit.
I wonder how you have taken this further blow?

OLD HORATIUS

Sir, with deep grief – and yet with resignation.

TULLUS
Then your age and experience have served you well.   1460
Many have learned like you, from a long life,
How misfortune often follows happiness.
Few know like you how to apply that truth,
And some can find no strength when they most need it.
If you can find in my compassion for you
Some small support in what you now endure,
Be assured that my sympathy is quite as strong
As your personal grief. You have all my love – and pity.

VALERIUS
Sir! – Because heaven has assigned to kings
Its justice, and the power of all its laws,   1470
And as the State demands of all lawful princes
Reward for virtue, chastisement for crime,
Permit a loyal subject to remind you
That here you are pitying what you ought to punish.
May I –

OLD HORATIUS
Then are we to punish our country's saviour?

TULLUS
Let him finish, and we shall give him justice
As we do to all, at all times and everywhere –
It is how a king attains to god-like status.
I said: I pity you – that after such service,
Your son should stand in need of our royal judgement.   1480

VALERIUS
Then allow me, O great King, most just of kings,
To speak in this for all good citizens:
In no sense are we jealous of his honours.
If he has those, in abundance, his deeds deserve them,
You may heap more honours on him, and withdraw none –
We are all still prepared to join in the praise.
But since he was capable of such a crime,
Let the conqueror triumph, and the criminal die!
If you wish to reign wisely, you should curb his rage

And save the rest of Rome from his violent hands; 1490
It's a matter of their safety, or their ruin.
The war took such a grim and deadly course,
And marriage ties, while our nations lived at peace,
Had so often joined together our two peoples,
That very few Romans would not have been involved
In the death, on the other side, of a son-in-law,
Or a brother-in-law, and were compelled to weep
Out of personal grief while the State of Rome rejoiced.
If what I say wrongs Rome, and his victory
Entitles him to punish such tears as crime, 1500
Whose blood will this brutish conqueror not shed
If he does not spare the tears of his own sister?
If he cannot forgive the overwhelming pain
The death of a lover stirs in a woman's heart
When – just before the nuptial torch is lighted –
She sees all her hopes go with him to the grave?
He brought Rome victory – now he is Rome's master,
With rights of life and death over us all,
And our less than virtuous lives will last no longer
Than he pleases himself, in his mercy, to allow. 1510
I might further add, still thinking of Rome's interests,
That such an act was unworthy of a man:
I could ask that they show you, so you might all see,
That last achievement of his conquering sword.
You would see her poor blood leap out to accuse
The cruelty of one who had been her brother,
You would be moved to horror beyond words
At the sight of the youth and beauty he cut down.
– But I do not wish to move you by verbal arts.
Tomorrow you perform the sacrifice: 1520
– Do you think the gods, who avenge innocent lives,
Will accept the incense from a parricide's hand?
Such profanity will bring down their wrath on you!
You should think of him as an object of their hatred,
And like us, realise that in those three combats
Rome's destiny decided, and not his sword.
Those very gods who gave him his victory
Allowed him, that same hour, to defile its glory,
So that his great courage and noble striving

Could in one day bring him victory – and death.   1530
Sir, your wise judgement must decide this question.
In this place Rome's first fratricide occurred –
His deed, and heaven's anger, should make us tremble.
Save yourself from his sword, and fear the gods!

TULLUS
                                        Horatius,
Defend yourself.

HORATIUS
                    What good will that achieve?
You know what I did, you have heard everything,
Your judgement of it will decide my fate.
– Sir, it is wrong to question a king's opinion:
The most blameless man becomes a criminal
When he appears so to his sovereign lord.   1540
It is a crime to make excuses to him;
Our blood is the King's property, to use
As he wants. We should know, when he takes away our lives,
That he does not do that except in a just cause.
I await your verdict and must be ruled by it.
Others love life, but I must hate my own.
I do not condemn Valerius's passion:
He loved the sister, and must accuse the brother.
Today my deepest wishes accord with his.
He demands my death, and I want it equally,   1550
But there is one point that divides the two of us:
The death I suffer must safeguard my honour,
And though both of us intend that I should die,
He seeks to defame my glory, and I to save it.
Sir, it is rarely that the chance occurs
For a noble soul to show all its qualities.
As the hour decides, it may achieve much, or little,
And seem either strong or weak to those looking on.
The people see only the surfaces, and judge you,
Crudely, by the results of what you do;   1560
They expect you to preserve the same public face –
You have done miracles, so you always must!
After some solid, proud, sublime achievement,

Anything less resplendent disappoints them:
It has to be equalled, each time and everywhere.
They don't think to ask if one could then do better,
Nor will they, with no new miracle to admire,
Realise the courage was there, but not the chance.
Their injustice wears down famous reputations,
The first success is not equalled by the second,   1570
So, if your fame has been exceptional
And you want to preserve it, you should let it rest there.
I shall not boast of my exploits in the war.
Your Majesty, you yourself saw my three combats:
Nothing like that could happen a second time,
No other occasion could ever compare with that,
And after such feats of arms, my famous courage
Could only strive after second-rate success.
If I wish my memory to be glorious,
Then death alone, today, can preserve my name   1580
It should have come in the hour of victory,
Seeing that I have now outlived my honour . . .
A man like me sees his reputation tarnished
In running the risk of even the slightest shame.
My own hand might have rescued me from that,
But without your word my blood could not dare to flow:
It belongs to you, your warrant is required,
And it would be theft to shed it otherwise.
Rome does not lack for courageous warriors,
Enough, without me, to uphold your mighty name –   1590
I ask Your Majesty to dispense with me,
And if all I have done deserves some recompense,
Allow me the right, O King, with my victor's sword
To die, for my glory's sake – not for my sister.

V.3 Tullus, Valerius, Old Horatius, Horatius, Sabina

SABINA

Sir, listen to Sabina, and find in her
The deep grief of both a sister and a wife.
She kneels down at your sacred feet in mourning

For three brothers' deaths, and fearing for her husband.
I am not wanting by means of artifice
To save a guilty man from the hand of justice.   1600
Whatever he did for you, treat him as guilty,
And punish this noble criminal – but through me,
Letting my own poor blood pay for all his guilt.
It would not mean just that a different victim suffered,
Or that you showed an unjust pity for him –
It would take the dearer half of his life away!
The bond of marriage and his abundant love
Mean that he lives more in me than in himself,
And if you consent to let me die today,
He will suffer more by my death than by his own.   1610
The death which I demand – which I must have –
Will intensify his anguish and end mine.
Your Majesty: consider my suffering,
And the grievous plight in which I find myself:
The horror of holding in my arms a man
Whose sword has ended my three brothers' lives!
Then, also, the blasphemy of hating one
Who has saved us all, king, Rome and family!
To love a hand stained by my brothers' blood,
And not love him who preserved our liberty!   1620
Sir, you yourself deliver me from the crime
Of loving him – and denying him my love!
My hand could give me what I demand of you,
But your sentence of death would be a favour.
That death would in the end be sweeter to me –
Then I could free my husband from all shame,
Then I could, with my blood, appease the anger
Roused in the gods by his over-violent courage,
Then I could bring some peace to Camilla's shade
And save for Rome the noblest of her defenders.   1630

OLD HORATIUS

(To the King)
I need, sir, to answer Valerius's case.
My children combine with him against their father,
All three wish my destruction, and for no reason
Set themselves against the one son left alive.

(To Sabina)
First you – putting your grief above your duty.
You wish to leave your husband and join your brothers.
Go then and seek advice from their noble shades:
They died for Alba, and gave their lives happily:
Since heaven decreed that Alba should be conquered,
If any feelings survive us after death,   1640
Its downfall should seem far less harsh to them
When they see the honour Rome achieves with it.
All three would reject the sorrow that afflicts you,
The tears in your eyes, the very sighs you breathe,
Your horror of your own courageous husband.
– Be their sister. Do your duty, as they did theirs.
(To the King)
Valerius's anger cannot touch her husband.
A passionate impulse never was a crime,
And praise is due, rather than penalties,
When that impulse is a courageous one.   1650
To sing the praises of our enemies,
Cursing our side in rage for killing them,
To hope that disaster will bring down our State –
These are crimes indeed, and these are what he punished.
His love of Rome, alone, moved him to strike.
Had he loved Rome less, he would be innocent.
– But what have I said? He *is*. This father's hand
Would have punished him already if he were guilty.
I would know how to use that absolute power
Given to me as a father by the law.   1660
I love honour, and I cannot stoop so low
As to suffer crime, and outrage, in my own blood.
On that, I can call Valerius as my witness.
He saw the welcome my anger had stored up
When I knew only one half of what had happened,
When I thought my son had fled, and betrayed Rome.
Who gave Valerius care of my family?
Who gave *him* the right to avenge my daughter?
What makes him take a greater interest
In Camilla's just death than even her father takes?   1670
Should we fear that, after her, others will be murdered?
– Sir, we need only worry about the shame

Of those closest to us – whatever others do
Should not make us blush if it isn't our concern.
(To Valerius)
Yes, you may weep, even though Horatius sees it.
Only the crimes of his own blood interest *him*.
No one born outside it can ever insult
Those immortal laurels that surround his brows.
You sacred wreaths! – which some would reduce to dust –
You can protect my son from heaven's thunder.   1680
Will you abandon him to the shaming blade
Which falls on the guilty from the headsman's hands?
And, Romans, will you see condemned a man
Without whom Rome would not today be Rome?
Would you have a Roman mar the great renown
Of a warrior who made your name so glorious?
Speak, Valerius. If you would have him die,
Suggest a fit place for his execution.
Somewhere inside those walls, still echoing
With several thousand voices praising his deeds?   1690
Or outside? – In the middle of that plain
Where the blood is still warm on three brothers' wounds?
Among their graves? On the same field of honour
That saw his valour and our victory?
He could only die on ground where men praise his glory;
Inside or outside these walls, it is the same;
They will all oppose this attempt of your jealous love
To stain our day of triumph with his blood.
Alba itself will not suffer it to happen,
And Rome will prevent it with her tears.   1700
(To the King)
You can forestall them, sir. With a just verdict
You may truly serve the interests of Rome.
What he has done for her he can do again –
Once more deliver her from a hostile fate.
Sir, make no concessions to my age and weakness.
I was today the father of four children.
Three of them died, for Rome, on this one day.
I have just one left. Let him live, for Rome.
Let him still support her walls with his mighty strength –
And let me finish with this appeal to him: 1710

(To Horatius)
Horatius, don't think the vulgar multitude
Ever has the final word on a hero's name.
Often its thunderous voice sends up great noise,
But in a moment it will have died away,
And whatever it may add to our reputation
Will have vanished again, in no time, like a mist.
Only to kings, great men, and noble spirits
Is it given to see the worth in our least actions.
It is they alone who award us real glory,
And guarantee that the mightiest names survive.   1720
Be worthy of this house, and among them
Your name will live as great, illustrious, famous,
Even if less high and brilliant moments come,
And the hopes of the ignorant crowd are not fulfilled.
Do not hate your life! Live, now – for me at least,
To go on serving your country and your king.
– Sir, I have said too much; but it all concerns you,
And all of Rome has spoken through my words.

VALERIUS

Sir, permit me –

TULLUS
Nothing more, Valerius.
Your arguments are not cancelled out by theirs,   1730
Their forcefulness is wholly clear to me
And your reasoning still vivid in my mind.
This terrible deed, done almost before our eyes,
Offends against nature and grieves the gods themselves.
It is said he acted on a passionate impulse:
That cannot serve to legitimise a crime;
On that point even the gentlest laws agree,
And if we abide by them, he deserves to die.
On the other hand, if we wish to name him guilty
Of a grave, appalling, inexcusable crime –   1740
Well, the hand that held the sword made us, today,
The undisputed master of two kingdoms.
If we hold two sceptres, Rome's – and Alba's now –
It speaks most eloquently in his favour.

But for him, we should be obeying, not laying down, laws –
As a subject, where we are now twice over king!
Good citizens everywhere fulfil their duty
By a humble loyalty towards their princes.
All can love their kings, but not everyone
Can save his country by acts of heroism.   1750
The skill and strength to render a throne secure
Are gifts that heaven awards to very few;
Such servants are the power that upholds monarchs –
And such men therefore stand above all laws.
Let the laws be silent! – Let Rome conceal the truth
She has known about Romulus ever since her birth,
Let her ignore in this warrior who saved her
What she ignores in the founder of our State.
You may live, Horatius, too great-hearted warrior:
Your loyalty sets your glory above your crime.   1760
Your zealous passion led to your offence,
But the cause was noble. We shall pass by the crime.
Live, to serve Rome – but in friendship with Valerius.
There must be no anger or hatred between you two,
And whether he argued out of love or duty,
See that you treat him without bitterness.
Sabina – listen less to your urgent sorrows,
And drive all weakness from your generous heart.
By drying your tears you will show yourself to be
A sister worthy of the men you mourn.   1770
– But tomorrow we owe the gods a sacrifice,
And heaven will not look kindly on our prayers
If, before the offering is made, our priests
Have not found means of purifying him.
His father will arrange it; and may easily
Appease Camilla's shade at the same time.
We pity her; and, conscious of her harsh fate,
Shall grant what her loving spirit would desire:
Since passions of the same strength, on the same day,
Consumed these two and took each life away,   1780
Let this same day which saw each piteous death
See them made one in the same Roman earth.

Notes

I.1.39-44. In the first book of the *Aeneid* (I.275-93), Jupiter prophesies to Venus that Rome will become great through military conquest and will ultimately rule the world. See also Old Horatius, III.5.987-91.

I.1.51. 'Pillars of Hercules': the Straits of Gibraltar. Lines 47-51 contain a deliberately anachronistic reference to contemporary French hostilities with Habsburg Spain and Austria, thus drawing together the depiction of Rome's first steps to universal empire and France's military ambitions in Europe in 1640.

I.1.52-5. Romulus and Remus were twin sons of Mars, god of war, and of Rhea Silvia, an Alban princess. Since Rhea was a vestal virgin, she and her children were condemned to be drowned in the Tiber. The babies survived to be suckled by a she-wolf and brought up by a shepherd who had found them. On later discovering their true identity, Romulus and Remus killed the usurper of the throne of Alba and re-established their grandfather Numitor. Subsequently they decided to build a city of their own but, in a quarrel over where to place its walls, Romulus killed Remus and buried him beneath the walls of his new city of Rome.

I.2.191. The Aventine was one of the seven hills of Rome. It was named after Aventinus, King of Alba, who was buried on it.

I.2.193. Apollo was the patron god of divination, most famously worshipped at Delphi, where the Oracle, in the person of the priestess, was consulted.

II.5.533, 571. In these lines, in the first edition of 1641 and subsequent editions including that of 1657, Camilla and Curiatius address each other as *ma chère âme*. In the 1660 edition they address each other by their names, for by then such tender familiarities were considered inappropriate to the dignity of tragedy. Later changes of sensibility and twentieth-century taste justify reinstatement of these original expressions of affection in the present translation.

II.8.697-8. A recollection of the Sabine women who had been abducted into marriage with their Roman captors (c. 755-50 BC). They threw themselves between the opposing armies of their Alban fathers and Roman husbands and so averted further bloodshed. Sabina's own name similarly recalls this, as do her words at III.2.776-8.

III.3.843-6. This reference to the divinely sanctioned king's special relationship to God is another seventeenth-century French anachronism in the play's Roman historical context. As with Sabina's earlier reference to the contemporary theatre of European hostilities (I.1.47-51), it has the effect of pointing up the relationship between the drama and seventeenth-century French political actuality.

IV.5.1291-4, 1305-18. Of Camilla's two curses, one will come true at once with the disgrace of Horatius. The second looks forward to the sacking of Rome by the Goths and Vandals in the fifth century AD and to the ruination of Rome's ancient monuments so apparent by the seventeenth century.

V.2.1532-3, V.3.1755-6. These closing references to Romulus's murder of Remus recall Sabina's opening reference at I.1.52-5.

V.3.1679-80. Ancient superstition had it that the laurel wreath protected its wearer against lightning, and so from the thunderbolts of divine retribution.

V.3.1766. See Appendix.

The Original Ending of *Horace*

In the first edition of 1641 and subsequent editions including that of 1657, Tullus left the stage after telling Horatius to bear no grudge against Valerius (V.3.1766). Julia was left alone to speak an epilogue in three quatrains, which once again stressed the obscurity of the gods' purposes in pointing out that the oracle had spoken unexpectedly true:

[TULLUS]
See that you treat him without bitterness.
(Exit; all follow except Julia.)

V.4 Julia

JULIA
Camilla, heaven warned you yesterday
About the tragic outcome it designed –
And yet its words were chosen to lead astray
Even the sharpest, most enlightened mind.

It seemed to say your wedding-day was nearing,
It seemed to grant your prayers – but what it said
Hid from us all your unexpected dying;
It spoke the truth – and yet we were misled.

At last, in answer to your fervent prayer,
For Alba and for Rome peace has begun;
And unkind fortune cannot touch you where
You and your Curiatius lie as one.

In 1660 Corneille suppressed this closure, in order to meet the requirement that the final destiny of all the principal characters should be made clear to the audience. Thus Tullus completes the play with extra lines which counsel Sabina and call for ceremonies to thank the gods and purify Horatius, as well as the joint obsequies of Camilla and Curiatius.

Historical Record

Legendary datings of Rome's early history

750 BC:	Romulus murders his twin brother Remus
21 April 753 BC:	Official date of the foundation of Rome
670 BC:	Triple combat between the Horatii and the Curiatii guarantees Rome's victory over Alba

Firm datings of later Roman history

1st and 2nd centuries AD:	Apogee of Roman power under Julian and Flavian emperors
410 AD:	Rome sacked by the Visigoths
455 AD:	Rome sacked by the Vandals

Corneille's historical sources

Livy, *The Early History of Rome (Ab urbe condita libri)*, I, 23-7
Dionysius of Halicarnassus, *Roman Antiquities*, II, 57

Further Reading

TEXTS

Corneille, *Horace* (Collection Livre de Poche), preface by J.-P. Miquel, notes by A. Couprié, Paris, Librairie Générale Française, 1986.

Corneille, *Horace*, ed. Christian Gouillart (Classiques Larousse), Paris, Larousse, 1990.

Corneille, *Horace* (Collection Univers des Lettres), ed. Pol Gaillard, Paris, Bordas, 1962 (repr. 1994).

Pierre Corneille, *Horace*, ed. P. H. Nurse, London, Toronto, Wellington, Sydney, G. G. Harrap, 1963 (repr. Nelson, 1986). An edition for English readers, which uses the text of the first edition, and has a useful introduction and glossary.

Pierre Corneille, *Oeuvres complètes*, ed. G. Couton, 3 vols, Paris, Bibliothèque de la Pléiade, 1980-7. Major French edition, substantially annotated; vol. I contains *Le Cid* and *Horace*, and a useful dossier on the *Querelle du Cid*, mentioned in the Introduction.

SEVENTEENTH-CENTURY BACKGROUND

Some of the less recent works listed are currently out of print but should be available in libraries.

W. D. Howarth, H. M. Peyre and J. Cruickshank, *French Literature from 1600 to the Present*, London, Methuen, 1972. Opening chapter by Howarth.

G. Brereton, *French Tragic Drama in the Sixteenth and Seventeenth Centuries*, London, Methuen, 1973.

J. C. Tournand, *Introduction à la vie littéraire du XVIIe siècle*, Paris, Dunod/Bordas, 1970 (new ed. 1984).

The Cassell Guide to Literature in French, ed. V. Worth-Stylianou, London, Cassell, 1996. Contains a short chapter on the seventeenth century.

GENERAL STUDIES OF CORNEILLE

P. J. Yarrow, *Corneille*, London, Macmillan, 1962. An introductory study in which the main interest of Corneille's work is held to lie in its close observation of contemporary 'reality'.

R. J. Nelson, *Corneille, His Heroes and Their Worlds*, Philadelphia, University of Pennsylvania Press, 1963. Argues against the existence of a tragic vision in Corneille's output.

Claude Abraham, *Pierre Corneille*, New York, Twayne, 1972. A basic introductory study.

Gordon Pocock, *Corneille and Racine: Problems of Tragic Form*, Cambridge, Cambridge University Press, 1973. A comparative study seeing Corneille, not entirely convincingly, as a forerunner of later naturalistic drama.

Louis Herland, *Corneille* (Collection Ecrivains de Toujours), Paris, Seuil, 1986. A very useful general introduction, admirably illustrated and with an excellent chronology and choice of extracts.

David Clarke, *Pierre Corneille: Poetics and Political Drama under Louis XIII*, Cambridge, Cambridge University Press, 1992. Argues the case for Corneille as an author of political tragedy.

Roy C. Knight, *Corneille's Tragedies: The Role of the Unexpected*, Cardiff, Cardiff University of Wales Press, 1992. A short study of Corneille's craft.

ON *HORACE*

Several of the above studies of Corneille contain chapters devoted entirely to *Horace*, as do a number of the works in French listed in the notes to the Introduction. But see also:

Harold C. Ault, 'The Tragic Genius of Corneille', *Modern Language Review*, 45 (1950), pp.164-76.

William H. Barber, 'Patriotism and Gloire in Corneille's *Horace*', *Modern Language Review*, 46 (1951), pp. 368-78.

C. J. Gossip, 'Tragedy and Moral Order in Corneille's *Horace*', *Forum for Modern Language Studies*, 11, 1975, pp. 15-28.

Roy C. Knight, *Corneille 'Horace'* (Critical Guides to French Texts 4), London, Grant & Cutler, 1981. Quotations in French, line-numbered.

W. J. Dickson, 'Corneille's Use of Judicial Rhetoric: The Last Act of *Horace*', *Seventeenth-Century French Studies*, 10 (1988), pp. 23-9.

JOHANN WOLFGANG VON GOETHE

Torquato Tasso

A version by Alan Brownjohn with Sandy Brownjohn
Introduction by T. J. Reed

A play about the moral and social problems of being a patron and being patronised. In the confrontation between artist and statesman at the cultivated court of Ferrara (symbolising Weimar), Goethe's own experience is fashioned into universal conflicts: between dream and reality, imagination and reason, liberty and the constraints of civilisation. This translation was commissioned by and performed at the National Theatre.

'The claustrophobic atmosphere Goethe creates by confining his Romantic character to a Classical play makes the work structurally a metaphor of its own theme. The translation catches the breathless spirit of Tasso's visionary soliloquies within a loose blank verse format and manages to contrast this language with the more regular and epigrammatic iambic pentameter of the courtly characters he chafes against.'

Stephen Plaice, *Times Literary Supplement*

For a complete list of Angel Classics write to Angel Books,
3 Kelross Road, London N5 2QS